PRAISE FOR

THE 7-MINUTE
ADMISSIONS DECISION

"Sean Ma has years of experience in the field and *The 7-Minute Admissions Decision* shows he is truly an expert on the nuances of college admissions. There is an art to the underlying patterns and strategies that create successful college applications. These themes are hard to describe and often leave applicants and their families lost in the process. In his first book, Ma captures the essence of US college admissions, making this guide accurate and actionable for any student or family hoping to create a compelling application."

—Lucy Chechik
Former Admissions Officer, Stanford University

"Ma is invested in the application process and generally cares about students. He understands the value of education and specifically the goal of having a student find the right match at a college or university where they will academically and socially succeed. The process of applying to a highly selective US university is complicated, but Ma maps out a clear strategy for those students seeking admission in a competitive collegiate marketplace."

—Megan Colt
Former Admissions Officer, Carnegie Mellon University

THE
7-MINUTE
ADMISSIONS
DECISI✓N

MAKING EVERY SECOND COUNT TO GAIN ACCEPTANCE TO YOUR DREAM SCHOOL

SEAN MA

Advantage | Books

Published by Advantage Books, Charleston, South Carolina.
An imprint of Advantage Media.

ADVANTAGE is a registered trademark, and the Advantage colophon is a trademark of Advantage Media Group, Inc.

Printed in the United States of America.

10 9 8 7 6 5 4 3 2 1

ISBN: 978-1-64225-913-1 (Paperback)
ISBN: 978-1-64225-912-4 (eBook)

Library of Congress Control Number: 2023920272

Cover design by Lance Buckley.
Layout design by Analisa Smith.

This publication is designed to provide accurate and authoritative information in regard to the subject matter covered. It is sold with the understanding that the publisher is not engaged in rendering legal, accounting, or other professional services. If legal advice or other expert assistance is required, the services of a competent professional person should be sought.

Advantage Books is an imprint of Advantage Media Group. Advantage Media helps busy entrepreneurs, CEOs, and leaders write and publish a book to grow their business and become the authority in their field. Advantage authors comprise an exclusive community of industry professionals, idea-makers, and thought leaders. For more information go to **advantagemedia.com**.

This book is dedicated to all those who believe in the transformative power of education and the pursuit of dreams. To the admissions officers who generously shared their wisdom and guidance, and the college coaches whose passion for developing talent inspired these pages. To my family and friends, for their unwavering support and patience during the writing journey. To my advisors and mentors, your guidance and feedback were the compass that steered this work. And to the readers, who embark on this journey with me, may this book be a valuable companion on your path to college admissions and recruiting success.

With gratitude,
Sean Ma

CONTENTS

ABOUT THE AUTHOR

Sean Ma has helped countless students gain admission to Ivy League schools and other elite universities, such as Stanford, Caltech, Oxford, and Cambridge. He's the President of Shanghai Leighton School and the Founder of Ma Academy, an institution specializing in preparing top students for college. He holds bachelor's and master's degrees from Columbia University, with an additional master's degree from Cambridge University.

Sean's career began as a financial advisor, but his passion for education led him to transition into admissions counseling. With over fifteen years of experience, he has also supported numerous student-athletes in securing recruitment into top NCAA programs across various sports.

Currently residing in Asia, Sean pursues a balanced lifestyle of fitness, travel, and adventure—he is currently planning to fly a small aircraft through the continent. Most of all, he loves helping students make their college dreams come true.

INTRODUCTION

Dear Parents,

As a college admissions expert, the first question I'm always asked is, "When is the right time to start planning for college?"

My answer is always the same.

"Yesterday."

Luckily, the second-best time to start planning for college is right now—whether your child is six or sixteen. Since you are reading this book, you're already on the right track to help them achieve the future of their dreams, and if your child's plan includes attending a top college or university in the United States, you don't have any time to lose. Gaining admission to a top US school has never been more challenging and, to be honest, more confusing. I'm here to help you and your child navigate this process.

Maybe you've heard the horror stories of the class valedictorian with a stellar GPA and perfect test scores who got turned down by their first-choice school, and maybe even their second-choice school. Or the seemingly well-qualified student who received rejection letters from almost every school they applied to. Or the student who, despite doing "everything right," didn't even get into their "safety" school.

It happens.

The higher education universe has never been more competitive. A student can do "everything right," or at least what used to be considered "everything," and still not make the cut. This may make you wonder: if your child is not the valedictorian of their class, president of the student body, or captain of the football team, and you don't happen to have ten to twenty million dollars lying around to build their dream school a new science building, what does that mean for their future? Do they still have a chance of getting into the school of their dreams or even *any* top university in the US? Or do you need to seriously revise your expectations?

I wrote this book to answer these questions and many, many more.

My name is Sean Ma and I am in the business of helping students earn acceptance to top US colleges and universities. I am the Founder and CEO of Ma Academy and the President of Shanghai Leighton School—two institutions dedicated to preparing high-performing students in China (and around the world) for admission to US colleges and universities. Through my work placing my students in top private and public institutions across the US, I've learned exactly what it takes to navigate the American higher education landscape and come out on top. I've also experienced that landscape from the other side, as a student. I hold both a bachelor's and master's degree from Columbia University, and I earned my second master's in the UK, at the University of Cambridge. I was a proctor of Brigham Young University's independent study program and hold both a Massachusetts Educators' license and a private pilot's license (although that second one, admittedly, has very little to do with college admissions!).

For more than ten years in the business of admissions counseling, test preparation, and academic support, my team and I have helped hundreds of students gain admission to Ivy League schools such as Columbia, Yale, and Princeton; elite universities including Stanford, Caltech, and MIT; well-regarded state schools such as University of Michigan-Ann Arbor and University of California at Los Angeles (UCLA); and even top institutions outside the US including Cambridge and Oxford. I've worked with many student-athletes, guiding them through the recruitment process for NCAA programs in a variety of sports. Along the way, countless other students with a wide range of skills and interests have benefited from my counsel to make their dreams of a top-level US education a reality.

There is a good chance I can help your child too.

Part of the reason you may be confused about what it takes for a student to get into a top US college or university is that there is no direct, quantifiable answer. Unlike the schools in Asia or Europe, there is no set numerical formula or threshold a student must meet after which admission is essentially guaranteed. The only thing that's guaranteed when it comes to higher education in America is that getting into a top college has never been harder. In 2022, the acceptance rates at the eight Ivy League institutions were all less than 10 percent, with the most selective Ivies (Harvard, Yale, and Princeton) admitting less than 5 percent of applicants.[1] The well-regarded public University of California at Los Angeles (UCLA) admitted 9 percent of applicants,[2] while its well-regarded private rival, University of Southern Califor-

---

1   Crimson News Staff, "Ivy League acceptance rates 2012-2022," *The Harvard Crimson*, May 4, 2022, https://www.thecrimson.com/widget/2022/5/4/ivy-acceptance-rates-2012-2022/.

2   "Freshman Profile," Admission UCLA, accessed October 04, 2023, https://admission.ucla.edu/apply/freshman/freshman-profile.

nia (USC), admitted a slightly more generous 12 percent.[3] These schools all provide a single snapshot within the US higher education landscape, but the numbers are reflective of typical admissions rates at most highly ranked schools.

What this means for your child, and for you, is that getting into one of these schools will be difficult. But it's also possible if you have a *strategy*.

I wrote this book to provide you and your child with one that works.

With so many qualified students competing for so few spots, the average college admissions officer spends no more than fifteen minutes, and often as little as seven, deciding whether to admit your child to the school they represent. That's it. Less than a quarter of an hour will, essentially, determine your child's future. In a world where every student has a 4.0 GPA and near-perfect to perfect SAT and ACT scores, how can your child possibly stand out from the others? How can they cut through the clutter of the other applications and get an admissions officer to say "yes"?

Don't worry. We'll get to all that very soon.

If your child has their sights set on an elite US institution, you can safely assume they're going to be competing with many students with similar GPAs and similar test scores. And by similar, I mean similarly high, the more selective the school your child is considering, the higher their numbers need to be to warrant consideration. Once they meet those "basic" academic requirements, the key to standing out against an army of students who look similar on paper is to focus on and develop those qualities that make your child uniquely *themselves*. By helping your child curate a high school experience that demonstrates commitment to their passions and develops skills within

---

3   "Facts and Figures," USC, accessed October 4, 2023, https://about.usc.edu/facts/.

those areas, they will be able to tell their story in an application in a manner that sets them apart from the rest.

At Ma Academy, we help our students achieve this through what we call the "Two Chest Muscles and Six-Pack Abs" strategy. This process breaks down the college admission process into eight areas of focus. The two chest muscles represent the "heart" of a student's resumé: classroom grades and test scores. The six-pack represents the various other elements a student must develop to create a winning college application. This book will guide you and your student, step by step, through the same process we use with our students, so you master all eight of these crucial areas.

We'll start with the basics your child needs to prepare for this journey: Passion, Focus, and Going Deep. We'll talk about how helping your child choose the right course of study for *them* (as opposed to what worked for your friend's child who got into Princeton) will help them develop into an ideal candidate for admission to a top school. We'll crunch the numbers and discuss precisely what various schools expect from your child in terms of grades and test scores and share some of the techniques we use at Ma Academy to make sure they are up to snuff.

Once we've tackled those two basics, we'll move into the six-pack abs portion of the process, which will include the following:

1. Developing an *admission strategy* that includes deciding which schools your student will target based on how well those schools match with their skills, interests, and achievements;

2. Choosing an *application theme* your child will use to tell their unique story of what they have accomplished in high school and how they will contribute to their chosen school's community;

3. Deciding the *extracurricular activities* your child will commit to which will give them real-world experience that develops their passions, reflects their application theme, and advances their overall admissions strategy;

4. Optimizing your student's *course selection* to include classes that will meet (or exceed) admissions officers' expectations while fleshing out the story they are trying to tell;

5. Techniques for obtaining the strongest *recommendation letters*, from the right people, saying the right things to make your student's case; and finally,

6. Tips for writing *college essays* that clearly communicate who your student is, what matters to them, and why they are the right fit for the school of their dreams.

Throughout this book, I'll share the experiences of some of my real-life students (although their names will be changed to protect their privacy), as well as insights from current and former admissions officers about how they make their decisions. When you've finished reading this book, you and your child should know everything you both need to know to select a dream school (or schools), build a strong high school resumé, and craft an application that will clearly and concisely convey to admissions officers why they will be a welcome addition to their school's next freshman class.

I'm looking forward to helping them get there.

Best,

Sean Ma

CHAPTER 1

THE BASICS:

PASSION, FOCUS, AND GOING DEEP

From the time he was a little boy, Alan knew one thing—when he grew up, he was going to go to college in the United States. And not just any college.

He was going to go to Yale.

Alan knew this would be a big challenge, but it was not an unreasonable goal. From his earliest days in primary school, he was always at the top of his class, and his standardized test scores placed him far above his peers. He came from a family that valued education. His parents were successful professionals with advanced degrees, and his older sister was at Vanderbilt, a very selective private university in the United States. It was almost expected that Alan would go to a top American school. It was his natural next step.

Still, Alan knew Yale was a very selective school—even more selective than Vanderbilt. He knew he would have to prioritize his education. When he entered high school, he made a difficult, but he thought wise, decision.

He quit playing sports.

Alan loved basketball and tennis, and he was pretty good at both, but he knew he was not good enough to play at the college level. So, he reasoned, this would just distract from his academics. He also said "goodbye" to his hobby of writing comic books. Alan thought there was no time for childish games if he was going to get into Yale. He had to focus on studying. And after eliminating every other activity from his schedule, that's almost all Alan did. Every hour which he would have spent playing tennis, basketball, or doodling comic book characters was dedicated to studying. He studied for his regular classes and took additional advanced courses in math and science, learned multiple languages, and added several history and economics classes to his already-packed academic schedule. On top of that, he took years of test prep courses for the SAT, the ACT, the English Language placement test, and the American Mathematics Competition Test. It was, as you might imagine, a lot of studying.

But it was worth it. After all, it was for *Yale*.

All of Alan's hard work appeared to pay off. His GPA was unblemished by even a single A-minus. His test scores were equally stellar. He was, at least on paper, pretty much perfect. He completed his application to Yale and sent it off, eagerly awaiting the day his acceptance letter would arrive and he would begin planning his move to the States.

But Alan never received an acceptance letter.

He was rejected.

How could this have possibly happened???

Why would Yale reject a student like Alan, who was clearly more than qualified and wanted to be there more than anything in the world?

The Lay of the Land

I set my sights on attending college in the US because when it came to higher education, America was number one. It still is, no doubt about it. Not only are American schools internationally recognized, but they also offer a level of academic freedom that schools in most other countries do not. For example, when a professor assigns an essay question in the US, the student gets a prompt or a couple of prompts to choose from, and they can write whatever they want as long as it fits within broad parameters. In the UK, in addition to that prompt, there are a lot of details and very strict rules that a student must follow to complete the assignment. Instead of encouraging free thinking, the content of the essay is predetermined, before the student even begins to write.

The US also gives students the freedom to study what they want to study. They are free to explore subjects outside of their declared major, wait two years before even declaring a major, change their major, double, or even triple major, or finish both a major and a minor (or concentration). As long as they get the credits required for graduation, students in the US are free to choose their own educational path and follow it wherever it leads. This really matters, because when a student enters college, they're usually around eighteen years old. How many eighteen-year-olds know exactly what they want to be when they grow up? I know I didn't! US colleges are unique in offering students the freedom and flexibility to explore who they are and then become it. It's no surprise that talented students like Alan set their sights on American schools. The problem is, many of them don't know what American schools want from prospective students—especially these days.

College admissions in the US have changed dramatically since when you went to school. In the twentieth century, admission decisions were almost entirely based on hard numbers. If a student's GPA and standardized test scores met or exceeded a certain threshold, like Alan's certainly would have, they were admitted. If the grades or test scores weren't enough, the student was rejected. It was black and white, cut and dried. Students knew exactly what they needed to do to achieve their goals; it was enough to just study hard for the best grades and test scores. In countries other than the US, particularly Asian countries, this is still the norm.

For admission to US colleges and universities, grades and test scores are only the start.

This isn't to say grades and scores don't matter, but elite institutions could fill their class many times over with students with perfect GPAs and testing, so they must make decisions based on other qualifications. For example, according to Yale's website, the average SAT score of the incoming freshmen Alan was competing with was between 720 and 770 in English and between 740 and 790 in math; in other words, almost perfect.[4] The school website doesn't list their average GPA, but it regularly comes in above a "perfect" 4.0, which is possible because of how accelerated courses are weighted on a transcript.

The point I'm making is, when you look at the numbers, the students admitted to Yale were a lot like Alan. So why did those kids get into Yale when Alan did not?

There are a few reasons, but we'll start with the most obvious one: *selectivity.* The more desirable a college or university is, the harder it is to gain admission to that school. That inherent selectivity is part of what makes a school desirable. Even among the very top US colleges,

---

4   "What Yale Looks For," Yale University, accessed October 4, 2023, https://admissions.yale.edu/what-yale-looks-for.

there's a little bit of a range, with some schools admitting a significantly larger percentage of their applicant pool than others.

As I mentioned in the introduction, Ivy League schools have extremely low acceptance rates, with the Big Three (Harvard, Princeton, and Yale) occupying the most exclusive tier, along with other big-name schools such as Stanford and MIT. Just a handful of the schools on this list accept over 30 percent of the students who apply, with a few more in the 20 to 30 percent range. The vast majority of these top US schools accept under 20 percent of applicants, with many accepting less than 10 percent.

Yale, the school Alan applied to, is one of the toughest schools to get into. In 2021, its acceptance rate was just 4.35 percent, the lowest in the school's history.[5] The fact that a school only accepts a small percentage of applicants doesn't mean *your* child should not apply to that school, but it is an important piece of information to consider when formulating your child's admissions strategy. One way to increase your child's odds of acceptance is to find institutions with a "natural fit."

One way to do that is to see how your student compares to the students their target schools typically admit. Most US colleges, including most of the schools we're talking about, post detailed admissions information and statistics on their websites including facts like:

- the percentage of applicants admitted to their most recent class,

- where they come from,

- their average standardized test scores (if applicable),

---

5   Anika Arora Seth, "Yale accepts 4.35 percent of applicants, marking lowest acceptance rate in history," *Yale Daily News*, March 30, 2023, https://yaledailynews.com/blog/2023/03/30/yale-accepts-4-35-percent-of-applicants-marking-lowest-acceptance-rate-in-history/.

- their average GPA,

- intended majors,

- and more (hobbies, languages spoken, how many of their family members have attended college, etc.).

When you compare your child to the posted information, you can get an idea of how they stack up against the competition, and factor that into your strategy.

If your child is an international student like Alan, another important statistic is the percentage of students admitted from overseas. Overall, international students represented about 4.6 percent of the entire US student population during the 2020/2021 school year. Of those students, the vast majority came from China, followed by India, South Korea, and Canada.[6]

Some colleges and universities, especially public ones, offer limited seats in their class for international and out-of-state students. Local students often receive preferential admission at public colleges and universities in their home states. For example, 88.7 percent of the University of Texas at Austin's class of 2025 come from the state of Texas. 8.8 percent come from US states outside Texas, and 2.5 percent from outside the US[7] This is common at American public universities, but that doesn't mean your child has zero chance of attending one. It's just another factor to be aware of when formulating your strategy.

Speaking of strategy, many top schools are extra welcoming to foreign students. While Alan's dream school Yale admits under

---

6   Katharina Buchholz, "Where America's international students come from," *Statista*, November 16, 2021, https://www.statista.com/chart/20010/international-enrollment-in-higher-education/.

7   The University of Texas at Austin, "Explore Our Freshman Profile," Office of Admissions, accessed September 10, 2023, https://admissions.utexas.edu/explore/freshman-profile.

5 percent of applicants, 14 percent of their admitted class of 2026 comprise students attending high school outside the United States. Coming from overseas could have been a boost for Alan, but it wasn't enough.

Why not?

What Top Schools Really Want

If you look at the admissions information page on Yale's website, you'll see the following statement:

As we carefully and respectfully review every application, two questions guide our admissions team: "Who is likely to make the most of Yale's resources?" and "Who will contribute most significantly to the Yale community?"[8]

This offers a clue into why Alan failed to gain admission to Yale. We already know his grades and test scores were in line with his competitors, but the international students who were admitted must have done a better job of conveying that they would make the most of the school's resources and contribute something valuable to the school community. Alan's application failed to show Yale's admissions department who he was as a person, other than a hard-working, studious individual with a dream of attending Yale. He didn't appear to have a passion for anything beyond academic success.

That's not what Yale, or other top US schools, are looking for.

Top US colleges and universities aren't looking for students who just hole up in the library for four years as undergraduate students. Most of the students who apply to these schools are nerds, at least to some degree, but they are nerds with a passion for activities outside of

---

8   Yale University, "What Yale Looks For," Office of Undergraduate Admissions, accessed September 20, 2023, https://admissions.yale.edu/what-yale-looks-for.

the classroom too. What matters is not what they have in common, but what sets them apart as individuals.

Like Yale mentioned on their website, admissions officers are looking for students who will add to the school *community*. A community where everyone is exactly like Alan— meaning a bunch of people who study all day and night and never do anything else— wouldn't just be boring, it wouldn't function! This is why top schools want to attract a variety of high-achieving students to their campuses. Not just mathematicians, engineers, and scientists, but writers, artists, free-thinkers, athletes, and activists. Not just leaders, but followers, and individuals who march to the beat of their own drum.

> **WHAT MATTERS IS NOT WHAT THEY HAVE IN COMMON, BUT WHAT SETS THEM APART AS INDIVIDUALS.**

This is good news for your child. No matter who they are, the right school will only want them to be exactly that—*who they are.* Your job as a parent is to help your student figure out the best version of themselves and then bring that person to life, just like we do at Ma Academy and the Leighton School.

A Little More About Me

I never wanted to be a teacher. The teachers I had growing up in China were mean and *so* boring. They were knowledgeable, but they didn't know how to convey that knowledge to students in a meaningful way, at least not to me. So, I got a job with an international financial services firm, which was a dream come true and perfect fit until a client approached me with an unusual request.

His son had been struggling in school, to the point where he was failing. His principal assumed the poor kid wasn't smart enough for regular school and advised my client to investigate special education. My client was horrified. He knew I had multiple degrees and had gone to college in the US and UK, so he came to me. Was there anything I could do to help his son?

I'm always up for a challenge, so I agreed to try. I started tutoring the boy in every single subject—English, math, social studies, etc. — but I focused on making our sessions fun, interesting and memorable. And guess what? The boy learned. After only a couple of months, his grades skyrocketed from 20 percent to 30 percent to above 80 percent and even reached 90 percent.

"Damn," I thought, "this is something rewarding."

I had discovered my passion. I started tutoring more students until I basically had a business on my hands, and left financial services to pursue education full time. When I was too busy to accept more students, I hired people to help me and taught them my methods. As my students aged through high school, I realized they didn't just need help in math or English; they also needed someone to help them navigate the college application process. Most high schools have a college counselor, but those counselors serve a lot of students and don't have a lot of one-on-one time to spend with individual students, guiding them toward that perfect school and crafting the perfect application. Their job is to make sure all their students get into college. Not their dream college, not the best college or even the best fitting college—just *a* college.

I wanted to provide a different kind of college counseling—counseling for kids like me, who dreamed of attending a top-ranked school in the US So, I set off on a summer road trip across the States, meeting with college admission administrators throughout the country, learning how they make their decisions. Since that first trip, I have met with admission officers representing more than hundred top US colleges and universities. Again and again, they confirm what I mentioned earlier in this chapter. They're not looking for students with perfect GPAs and test scores (although those things couldn't hurt!). They're not looking for students who have performed dozens of hours of "community service" doing things they neither care about nor have an aptitude for.

What matters is that, beyond meeting the basic qualifications, a student can demonstrate a *passion* for something beyond academics, *focus* their energy on that passion, and *go deep* into an aspect of that passion, making it an integral part of them.

Those three things (passion, focus, and going deep) distinguish an individual student from the pack of similarly qualified students. They not only provide a window into who the student is as a person, but they also give admissions staff an idea of how that student might add to the college community. That's the intangible thing that admissions officers are looking for in those seven minutes they spend viewing your child's application.

It's also the thing Alan failed to demonstrate.

The X-Factor

Let me explain. When I applied to Columbia University in New York, I had strong grades and test scores like most of my fellow applicants, and like Alan did. But I also had a differentiator. My real dream in life was to become a commercial pilot, but because I'm colorblind, that was not an option. However, my passion for flying was so strong that I earned my private pilot's license anyway—while I was still a teenager. This turned out to be my X-factor. It not only helped me stand out from every other applicant from China with good grades and test scores, but it also gave admissions officers a window into my personality. It showed I was determined, flexible, and focused, even when the odds were against me. Maybe even more importantly, it showed I cared about something beyond academics.

Now let's apply that thinking to Alan.

Had he continued to play one of the sports he loved through high school, who knows where his passion and focus could have taken him? He would have become a better player, leader, or coach. What if he continued drawing comics? He would have gained artistic, writing, and storytelling skills. How many other kids coming from overseas with good grades and test scores would have a profile like that? Chances are, Alan would have been the only one. He would have stood out from the crowd instead of blending in. And maybe, just maybe, he would have gotten into Yale.

What You (and Your Child) Can Do

As I mentioned at the beginning of the book, the best time to start planning for college is yesterday, within reason. In an ideal world, I generally recommend families have a first "real" discussion about college before the beginning of the student's freshman year of high school. Middle school is ideally an exploration phase, when your child should be trying a lot of different things to narrow down their interests and discover their skills. By freshman year, they need to make some decisions and concentrate their energy into one or two *passions*.

Keep in mind that your child's passion is not something you, as a parent, can or should determine. Maybe you've heard that kids who participate in writing competitions or kids who devote themselves to a social cause "do better" in the admissions process. In reality, your child is likely to "do better" at something they actually love doing. Your only job as a parent is to help them find that something, whatever it might be, and then do whatever you can to help them pursue it.

High school is the time for your child to *focus* on their passion. All their activities and elective classes should be connected to fueling that passion in some way, helping your child grow their skills and gain experience doing what they love. This should also start directing your child toward an *intended major*—and having one is an important part of a college admissions strategy.

SHOULD YOUR CHILD DECLARE A MAJOR ON THEIR APPLICATION?

Students in the US have the option of waiting until junior year to declare a major, and often apply to college as "undeclared" or "undecided." If you Google "applying to college undeclared," most articles written for prospective students and parents advise them against declaring a major, or at least claim that failing to declare a major will not hurt them in any way. I disagree. A student's intended major can be a big differentiator—especially if that major doesn't fit the profile typically associated with who they are as a student. For example, I worked with an Asian boy who was interested in both STEM and the humanities. I advised him to apply as a humanities major. Why? Because he would be one of many Asian boys applying to a STEM major. As a humanities major, he would already be setting himself apart. He followed my advice and he got into Stanford.

Ideally, your child should *go deep* in exploring their passion, taking it as far as they can possibly go. Whether that means spearheading a public-service initiative, competing in an athletic championship, making a movie, publishing a book or, in my case, getting a pilot's license, taking their passion to the limit will show that your child has the right stuff to succeed in a competitive college environment, and that they will bring something unique to their college community.

Next Steps

If you haven't already, sit down with your child and talk with them openly about what they love to do (not what you want them to love to do), and ways you can help them get better at doing it. Make sure your child's classes and activities are as aligned as possible with what they love. As their parent, you have the power to help your child go as deep as they can with their passion, developing their skills and talents to their maximum potential.

Passion, focus, and going deep are the essentials your child needs to have in place before they start the college application process. These three ideas will form the heart of the story within their college application. In the next chapter, we'll take a closer look at my process of building an application before attacking each of the eight components.

CHAPTER 2

THE PROCESS:

TWO CHEST MUSCLES AND SIX-PACK ABS

Back when I first started Ma Academy, I was into physical fitness. This was before I became a father, before I was running two schools, and before I was preparing hundreds of students for college each year, so I had a little more time for "self-care." I spent a lot of it at my local gym, in pursuit of physical fitness. I was there one day, in the middle of a crunch, when it suddenly hit me: *Getting ready to apply to a top US college is a lot like working out.*

Thus, the "Two Chest Muscles and Six-Pack Abs" method was born. I should probably explain...

When we exercise, many men put a lot of energy into their two chest muscles—the "pecs." The bigger and more "pumped-up" those chest muscles get, the more the average person can tell that a guy works out. It's fast, it's simple, and it's obvious enough to see through a shirt. That makes those two chest muscles a lot like those two long-standing pillars of (almost) every college application: grade point average (GPA) and test scores (ACT, SAT). While achieving high numbers in those two areas may not be as quick and easy as building chest muscles, it's not hard to figure out what to do and how to do it.

We've already established that while GPA and test scores are still important at most top US colleges and universities (although some schools are currently modifying their approach to standardized tests—more on that later), they're no longer the be-all and end-all when it comes to demonstrating a student's accomplishments or college readiness. They're only two parts of a much bigger picture, kind of like how chest muscles are only part of a fit body.

Well-developed chest muscles stand out, just like a perfect GPA or ACT/SAT score stands out. They can certainly get somebody that first look. But what happens when you look a little closer? Sometimes, a guy has big chest muscles, but when you lift his shirt to reveal his stomach, you might see something else: love handles, a beer belly, or the little pooch in the gut constituting the "dad bod." If you're in great shape, you're not going to be flabby around the middle. A *really* fit person is going to have six-pack abs because developing those muscles takes more work and finesse.

When you apply this logic to college, the six-pack abs represent those extra things that help your child demonstrate who they are as a person. For a student to get into a top American college today, they need a life of experiences that show they're a well-rounded, goal-oriented individual outside the classroom. In my program, we focus on the following six key areas:

1. admissions strategy;

2. application theme;

3. extracurricular activities;

4. course selection;

5. recommendation letters; and

6. college essays.

Those are the "six-pack abs" this book will help your student develop.

All eight of the elements I've mentioned in this chapter are essential, so let's take a closer look at the two chest muscles, grades, and test scores, first.

Building the Basics

These days, strong grades and test scores no longer mean your child *will* get into top a US school, but if they don't have these two fundamental elements, they *won't* get into a top US school. Grades and test scores are essential and must be in good shape before your child moves on to developing their six-pack.

How strong your child's academics need to be depends on which institutions your child wants to attend. A good first step to get a clear academic picture of an institution is to look at the kind of applicants that the school typically admits. As aforementioned, most schools list this information on their websites, but the best resource is something called a *Common Data Set.*

The Common Data Set provides detailed information about each college or university. It includes admissions data describing the typical admitted student academic record and test scores, information about required standardized testing, and what factors they consider most important in an application. In other words, a school's Common Data Set will give you a pretty good idea of what their admissions officers will be looking for when they make their seven-minute decision about *your* child.

To find the Common Data Set for a school your child is considering, just Google "Common Data Set" and the name of the college, and you'll uncover a treasure trove of information. These documents aren't always the most "reader friendly" as they include a lot of information unrelated to admission statistics, but once you move past those initial pages, I guarantee you will find some nuggets of information that you and your child will both find helpful.

For example, if you look at the 2021–22 Common Data Set for my alma mater, Columbia University, you'll learn some key facts. For example, Columbia University considered the rigor of an applicant's secondary school record, their class rank, and their GPA as "very important" when making admissions decisions, but standardized test scores were just "considered." Forty-four percent of applicants submitted SAT scores, while 29 percent submitted ACT scores, and of those applicants who were admitted, 93 percent had SAT scores in the 1400–1600 range, and 99 percent had an ACT score of thirty or higher.[9]

That information provides more than a snapshot of the typical student Columbia admits. It also provides vital information you and your child can use to formulate their admissions strategy. For example, the three pieces of information I shared from Columbia University's Common Data Set reveal that if your child's test scores are not competitive, they may not be penalized if they don't submit their scores—as well as what counts as a competitive score at that school. It's just one example of the kind of information you can get from the Common Data Set and how you might put it to use. There

---

9   Columbia Engineering, "Common Data Set Columbia College Engineering 2021-2022," Office of Planning and Institutional Research, Columbia University, September 9, 2022, https://opir.columbia.edu/sites/default/files/content/Common%20Data%20Set/Common%20Data%20Set%20Columbia%20College%20Engineering%202021-2022.pdf.

are potentially dozens more tidbits as the entire document is forty-three pages long! Each school's Common Data Set should give you a clear idea of whether that school is within reach for your child at this moment, and where, if they have their heart set on that school, they need to focus their efforts to improve.

CHEST MUSCLE 1: GPA

After examining the Common Data Sets for your child's target schools, one thing will become clear: the higher your child's grades are, the easier their path to their dream school will be. However, there is a little bit of wiggle room when it comes to grades. If your child takes the hardest courses offered in their school, like honors, Advanced Placement, or International Baccalaureate classes, and they get a B in one of those classes, that's actually preferable to an A in an "easy" or "standard-level" course. Regardless of how your child's school weights their GPAs, admissions officers will look at the rigor of your student's courseload and consider that as a factor. Columbia University certainly does, at least according to their Common Data Set survey.

As a parent, your goal is simple: help your child earn the highest grades in the hardest classes while still incorporating their passions. This does not mean doing their work for them. It's essential that your child learn *how to learn*. If they don't and somehow stumble into a top school, they won't survive their first semester. That means making sure they do the basic stuff now:

1.   Finish their homework

2.   Participate in class

3.   Earn high marks on exams and projects

4. Cultivate a good relationship with their teachers

I want to take a moment to make a point about the fourth item on that list. There is a common misconception among international students that it doesn't matter what they do during the school year because the only thing that matters is their score on the final test. American schools aren't like that. In America, everything that happens in the classroom counts. If you are American, you know this. If you are international, and your child is interested in a US school, they should start cultivating those relationships with their teachers now.

If your child is doing everything they should be doing and their GPA isn't on par with the students being admitted to their dream school, now is the time for you to intervene. First, pull their focus back to the basics. If they're involved in a lot of activities outside of school, it's time to cut back, not eliminating hobbies completely like Alan did in Chapter One, but cut back on some. Activities matter, but only once the fundamentals of strong grades and test scores have been developed. Activities aren't enough to save an application if your child's grades aren't high enough to make the cut in the first place. If your student is struggling with any subject, or even multiple subjects, don't wait. Have them reach out to their teacher for help as soon as you recognize the problem, and if things don't improve, hire a tutor. I know from my own experience working as a tutor that personal, one-on-one attention really does help kids learn. The sooner you act, the sooner you can help your child fix the problem and move on to the aspects of their application that will set them apart from all those other kids already earning good grades.

If your child's grades are on track, my advice is to keep doing what you're doing, keep them doing what they're doing, and, in addition to the test prep details I'm about to get into, transition your focus to their six-pack.

CHEST MUSCLE 2: STANDARDIZED TESTS

The ACT and SAT used to be essential to every college application. However, as I mentioned earlier in this chapter, standardized test scores are no longer mandatory to apply to some top US colleges and universities. This is a recent development, reflecting a response to criticism that standardized tests discriminate against low-income students and students of color in the US. Now, different schools are implementing different policies regarding standardized testing, which fall into three basic categories:

1. "Test optional" schools allow applicants to submit test scores for consideration if they choose to.

2. "Score Choice" schools allow students to submit their best test scores.

3. "Test blind" schools do not consider standardized test scores even if they are submitted.

This means that instead of just preparing for tests, you and your child need to prepare a testing strategy that includes:

1. Deciding which test(s) to take

2. Studying to prepare for those test(s)

3. Taking practice tests

4. Deciding how many times to take a test

5. Deciding whether to include test scores on an application

These are all important considerations for your child to get the most benefit from standardized testing. Let's break them down, step by step.

Choosing Which Test

The SAT and ACT are similar, but test students in slightly different ways. I could try to explain exactly how these exams differ, but the best way to know what is right for your child is simple: have them take a practice test for both exams.

If your child's score on one test is demonstrably higher, or they feel more comfortable taking one test than another, that's where they should concentrate their test prep efforts. If your child feels confident taking either test, they can choose, or prepare for and take both tests and decide which one to submit to schools when their scores come in.

Test Prep

Once you know which test your child will be taking, they can begin to prepare. That might mean enrolling in the appropriate online or in-person test-prep courses, working with a tutor specifically trained to prepare them for the test they are taking, joining a study group, or some combination of the above.

I recommend your child begin formal test prep earlier than their school counselor might advise. My students start ACT and/or SAT prep the summer before eleventh grade and take the test for the first time in the first semester of eleventh grade. That gives them time to determine which test they prefer, do more prep in areas where they are weaker, and, if necessary, take the test again to try for a better score. By the way, reading recreationally (yes, just for fun) is one of the best ways to prepare for the language portion of standardized tests.

If your child is an international student, they will also need to demonstrate English proficiency by taking the Test of English as a Foreign Language (TOEFL) or International English Language Test System (IELTS). These tests shouldn't require a ton of studying as they're basic assessments of your child's English reading, writing, speaking, listening, and comprehension skills. These exams don't go nearly as deep as the ACT or SAT, but if your child can't get a passing score on this test, it's probably wise to rethink their plan to apply to a top US school.

I recommend starting to prepare for the English proficiency test in ninth grade, with the goal of finishing the prep, taking the test, and receiving a good enough score in tenth grade. This way, your child will be ready to switch their focus to ACT or SAT prep sooner.

Practice Tests

Some students have no problem taking tests, while others are uncomfortable sitting for long exams or get anxious about standardized testing. I believe practice makes perfect when it comes to *taking* tests, because the less your child is worried about process, the more they can focus on doing their best. At Ma Academy, that means having our students sit for practice tests that mimic the actual test conditions. They take their practice tests in a "test condition room," multiple times, so it becomes muscle memory. This is proven to help eliminate pre-test jitters and gives students extra confidence.

You probably don't have your own "test condition room," but you can still do a few things to mimic those test conditions on your own. Arrange for your child to take the practice test in an empty classroom or library where there are no distractions. They should only bring the same materials they will bring to the actual test and nothing else, except a stopwatch to keep time (not their phone, since those can be used to cheat and are therefore prohibited!). This extra step will help your child prepare for test day.

Deciding When to Stop

Standardized tests can be taken multiple times, but it's important to make each time your child takes the ACT or SAT count. After the second time, it's unlikely your student will perform significantly better.

Since so many schools no longer require standardized tests, better for your student to use that time pursuing their passion or improving their grades. Remember, top schools are looking for curious, passionate, well-rounded students, not test-taking machines. If your child takes the SAT or ACT once and gets an almost-perfect score, congratulations! There is no need to waste precious time preparing and sitting for the exam again in hopes of a perfect score. Remember to factor that into your child's testing strategy.

Test Submission

Deciding which test to submit to a school is simple. Obviously, your child will want to submit the test with the highest score. If your child takes both the ACT and SAT and needs to choose, check the school's Common Data Set to see which score compares most favorably with the school's last incoming class, which test they favor (if any), and decide accordingly.

If your child is applying to a "test optional" school, check the school's most recent class's scores on their Common Data Set. If your student's score falls below the twenty-fifth percentile, and they are not a recruited athlete or have any other special talents, then don't report the score on the application.

That's all you need to know about the two chest muscles, so let's move on to the six-pack abs.

Building Your Child's Six-Pack

As I mentioned earlier in this chapter, when you're working out, developing six-pack abs is more challenging than building chest muscles. The muscles involved are harder to work, and seeing results requires time, dedication, and finesse. Plus, even after your child develops a six-pack, nobody will know it's there unless they take off their shirt and show it!

I'm not advocating for your child to strip down, but they will need to develop their six-pack if they hope to be a good candidate for a top college. Just like building abs, this will take effort, time, and the results won't be obvious unless your child can clearly communicate them to the admissions officers. My process is designed to help your child build their six-pack, resulting in a resumé that tells their story in a compelling way, setting them apart from the competition. We will take a deep dive into each of these elements over the remainder of this book, but for now, I'll give you a brief overview.

ADMISSIONS STRATEGY

Back in the day, an "admissions strategy" was to get the best grades and scores possible and apply to schools that accepted students with similar scores. Today, a good admissions strategy starts by identifying your child's passion, and builds everything else around it. Your child's admissions strategy should identify and target colleges and universities that will help them pursue their passion in some way. The college or university must offer a pathway to develop your child's passion into a profession, or at least open doors for further self-development and self-actualization. A good admissions strategy should account for how your child compares to the students their target schools admit and what those schools value.

APPLICATION THEME

Good college applications tell a story. This story can be anything from triumph over adversity, pursuit of a passion, or dedication to a cause. This story should present the big picture of your student's life, including their unique experiences, accomplishments, and values. These should be tied together to demonstrate what your child hopes to achieve in the future, allowing admission officers to get a sense of who your child is and why they will be a good addition to the school community. If that sounds like a tall order, don't worry, we'll get into detail about exactly how to accomplish this in Chapter Four.

EXTRACURRICULAR ACTIVITIES

Admissions officers care about what your student does outside of school and how they perform within those spaces. They want extra-curricular activities that align with a student's application theme; activities demonstrating commitment to their passions and depth of engagement. That means your child shouldn't sign up for a laundry list of random activities just for the sake of doing them. Activities should relate directly to the overall application theme and show how your child built their skills and experiences in their areas of passion (not areas where *you* think they should be passionate!). Don't try to think about what admissions officers want to see, as they want to accept different types of students to create a diverse student body.

What do I tell my students? Do what you love and love what you do!

COURSE SELECTION

In high school, your child should focus on courses that align with their passion, prepare them for their intended major, and challenge them to stretch and grow. They should demonstrate commitment to their education and excitement in the classroom, demonstrating how they are the type of student a future professor will want to teach.

When given flexibility in course selection, choices should reinforce the overall application theme.

RECOMMENDATION LETTERS

Top colleges will require at least one or two recommendation letters from teachers in core classes, college counselors, or other adult authority figures who can vouch for your child. Instead of waiting until the last year of high school to identify potential letter-writers, your child should be building relationships with their teachers from the beginning of their high school career. This way, if they want a recommendation later, they will feel comfortable requesting it knowing it will be a strong recommendation. They should be active in class and demonstrate leadership in their extracurricular activities, so they can get noticed by the adults in their life. When it is time to ask for a recommendation letter, your child should know how to subtly guide their recommender into giving the recommendation they want, making sure the recommender is aware of who they are as a person, their passions, intended major, and how the letter will fit within the broader application theme. We will cover how to fit this all into a letter in Chapter Seven.

COLLEGE ESSAYS

College essays typically include your child's "personal statement" and one or more supplemental essays. The fact that there are two (or more) of them is a good thing, because essays are your student's last, and best, chance to shine. Essays are where they can show their personality, express their passion, and tell their story, all while demonstrating their writing skills. A good college essay can put a positive spin on any weaknesses in an application, provide context for any failure, and paint a picture that highlights the very best aspects of your student. How can an essay do all that? I'll detail exactly how to accomplish all of this (and more!) in our final chapter.

Next Steps

Now is a good time to work on reinforcing your child's study habits. When your student is doing homework (especially if your child is younger, but it's never too late to start), don't watch TV or look at your phone. Instead, read a book. You'll be modeling a good habit for your child.

You can engage with your child while they do their homework if they need or want it, but don't get too engaged. Offer help when your child asks, or if you know they tend to get stuck, but don't stare over your kid's shoulder while they're writing an essay or working on some math problems (read your book instead!). The goal is for your child to find their answers on their own.

If your child struggles and you hire a tutor, make sure your child is still the one doing their homework, not the tutor. Students should always complete their homework to the best of their ability before the appointment, so they are aware of what they don't know. This allows the tutor to focus on helping them where they need it. Teach your child to be proactive: figuring out what they don't know and asking for help when they need it.

Now that you know how the two chest muscles and six-pack abs method works, let's dig deeper into the six-pack abs, beginning with how to develop an effective admissions strategy .

CHAPTER 3

AB WORKOUT #1:

ADMISSIONS STRATEGY

By the time she finished middle school, Sasha knew that there was a good chance that she would have the grades and test scores to get into a top college. She just had no idea where to start. She'd heard of schools like Harvard, Stanford, Duke, and MIT. She knew their names, reputations, and a little about where they were located. She also knew that they were very, very competitive. What Sasha didn't know was how to top her competition to get accepted beyond earning good grades and test scores.

Honestly, that's what a lot of students who dream of attending a top university do. Hope and hard work, however, are not really a *strategy*. These days, if your student hopes to get into a top US school, they're going to need one...as soon as possible. Luckily, I'm here to help you start formulating that strategy so it's ready to go when they start their freshman year of high school.

A college admissions strategy is basically just an informed, step-by-step approach to college planning that will boost your child's chances of getting into the right college *for them*. Those two words, *for them*, are crucial. Choosing a college or university is one of the most important decisions your child will make in their lifetime, yet too many kids (and parents) make that decision for the wrong reasons. They fixate on the name of a school or its perceived reputation without having any idea of what going to that school would be like, what it takes to get in, or if the school is even a good fit for their child and their life goals.

That's why it's essential for you and your child to develop an admissions strategy that will help them narrow their focus to the "right" schools. "Right" means schools that offer the programs that meet their interests and goals, provide the kind of environment where they will feel comfortable, and, of course, that your child has a reasonable chance of being accepted. Once they know which schools to focus on, they can fine-tune their strategy and do whatever they can (details to follow) to appeal to admissions officers at those specific institutions.

Creating Your Strategy

Basically, an admissions strategy should consider:

1. Your child's passions.

2. Colleges that will help develop your child's passions.

3. Colleges that fit your child's needs in other ways (size, culture, and location, etc.).

4. The average GPA and test scores of their incoming freshmen and how your child's numbers compare.

5. How many students a school admits from your region, especially if your child is an international student or applying out of state to a public university.

6. Areas where your student may fill a target school's need, such as interest in a specific major or possessing a particular talent or skill.

This chapter will take you through the process, step by step, of building an admissions strategy that will help your child create a standout application to the schools that are the best fit for them. We will use Sasha and her admissions strategy as an example, so keep in mind that your child's passions, skills and personal preferences will probably be different. The point is to provide you with an outline of the process for you to implement with your child.

STEP 1. START WITH PASSION

Finding the right college is ultimately about finding a school that will nurture your child's passions and help them progress toward a career and life they will love. To do that, you must help them narrow down their many interests to one or two areas they are passionate about and excited to focus on in high school.

Many high-achieving students like Sasha are "good at everything" kids who excel at most things they pursue, both in and out of the classroom. Being "good at everything" isn't a bad thing, but it also describes most students applying to top US colleges and thus is inherently not a unique differentiator. To get into a college where almost every applicant has a strong academic profile supported by many accomplishments, your student needs a *differentiator* to set them apart from the crowd. At Ma Academy, we help students turn their passion into their differentiator. You can do the same for your student.

As a parent, you can help your child discover their passion by paying attention to what they like to do and what they're good at doing. Talk with your student about what they like, what they value, and what they dream of doing when they grow up. Notice, these hopes and dreams might be different from what *you* like, value, or want your child to become. Offer them plenty of opportunities to explore whatever they want to explore throughout middle school. Then, when they're getting ready to start high school, sit down with them and help them choose which of their interests they would like to pursue more deeply.

When Sasha's parents had this conversation with her, they talked about what they knew she liked to do and was good at. She was the captain of her softball team, and loved drama, art, writing, math, and science. Her parents had seen her pursue and excel in all these areas over the years. Among all these interests, what did Sasha *really* care about? They asked her what she would do if she could do anything she wanted. Through this conversation, it became clear that Sasha was drawn to ending climate change.

That was Sasha's passion.

Sasha and her parents began to formulate an admissions strategy focused on supporting her passion. First, they narrowed down her many activities to a few that focus and deepen her experiences in that area. Sasha did not want to quit softball since she was good at it and really enjoyed the physical activity and the leadership opportunities associated with the sport. Her other activities, however, were fair game to discontinue to make time for her passion.

Instead of Drama Club, she joined her high school's Climate Action Club. Instead of writing short stories and poems, she volunteered with the communications team at her local chapter of Greenpeace, writing letters to elected officials and business leaders to advocate for environmental action. Her leadership skills led her to spearhead an initiative at her school encouraging students to bike or walk instead of driving. She used her artistic talents to create the poster advertising the initiative. Her focus paid off. Sasha began attending, and later speaking at, climate conferences. Here, she met leaders in her community who shared her passion for saving the world. When presented together in her application, these experiences showed admissions officers what sort of change-maker Sasha would become as a student on their campus.

STEP 2. DETERMINE WHICH SCHOOLS MATCH THAT PASSION

There's nothing worse than students focusing for years to get into the school they think they want to attend, only to realize that the school doesn't even offer the major they're hoping to complete. Just because a school has a great reputation does not mean it will be a great school for your child. The best way to avoid making this costly and hard-to-correct mistake is for your child to have a sense of what they want to do before they apply, and then research which schools offer the courses and majors that will allow them to do it.

This is not a difficult task. Every college publishes a course catalog listing all majors, minors, programs, and classes they offer. This is easily accessed on the college website. If your child doesn't know where to start, there are many books that can help them decide. The top-selling *Fiske Guide to Colleges* by Edward B. Fiske provides a comprehensive overview of more than 300 schools in the US and Canada, while *Colleges That Change Lives: 40 Schools that Will Change the Way You Think About Colleges* by Loren Pope and *The Hidden Ivies: 30 Colleges of Excellence* by Howard Greene focus on excellent schools that offer a transformative college experience and maybe a little more off the radar. Doing research ahead of time will help your child understand what schools will offer them the best opportunity to pursue their specific passion, as well as how they might fit into the college culture (more on that in a minute).

For Sasha, figuring out what schools to focus on meant first getting an idea of what a student interested in fighting climate change might study in college. Her online research revealed a variety of different paths to follow to turn her passion into a profession. If she wanted to focus on the science behind climate change, she could major in Climate Science or, more broadly, Environmental Science. She could learn to build solutions to climate issues through an Environmental Engineering or Sustainability Studies program. Sasha could also avoid STEM entirely, focusing instead on environmental governance and public communication with a Public Policy or Political Science degree.

Once she was aware of her options, Sasha's next step was to research which schools offered a bachelor's degree in one or more of these climate-focused programs. Her search yielded a broad range of colleges and universities across the US, including STEM schools like MIT and Columbia University, small liberal-arts schools including Swarthmore College and Pomona College, and a long list of well-regarded state schools, including the University of Michigan, Arizona State University, and University of California campuses at both Berkeley and San Diego.

All in all, there were more schools on Sasha's list of possibilities than she could possibly apply to. This will probably be the case for your student as well. The next step is narrowing that list to schools that will make your student happiest (and where they have a good chance of being admitted).

STEP 3. CONSIDER SCHOOL TYPE AND CULTURE

There are all kinds of great colleges and universities in the US, from prestigious Ivy League schools to world-renowned STEM schools, from small, private liberal-arts colleges to big, public universities. There are colleges and universities in every state, in big cities and small towns, in warm and cold climates. There are schools where students can design their own curriculum, and one highly regarded school, St. John's University, where every student follows the exact same program: the 100 "Great Books," in which they learn everything from math and science to religion and philosophy through those writings.[10] There are religious schools, schools with liberal-leaning culture, and schools with a more conservative ideology. Some schools are known for their athletic programs, some for their party scene, some for their well-connected alumni...the list goes on and on.

Naturally, some of these types of schools are going to be a better fit for your child than others. The next step is for you and your child to consider what kind of environment (or environments) they could be happy living and learning in and then narrow down their list to schools that fit those parameters.

In Sasha's case, she found a lot of schools on her list attractive for different reasons. She was flexible about where and how she wanted to live, the size of the school she wanted to go to, the campus culture, and more. This will probably be the case for your child as well. How should your child decide which schools on their list they will apply to? The next step is researching your child's favorite institutions to determine their likelihood of gaining admission.

STEP 4. CONSIDER THE SCHOOL'S REQUIREMENTS

Until this point, we've been focused on finding schools your child might want to attend. Now, we need to switch the focus to which

---

10   Saint Joseph's College of Maine, "Academic Programs," accessed January 30, 2023, https://www.sjc.edu/academic-programs.

schools might want to admit your child. This means looking at the school's admissions criteria and the profile of their most recent class of admitted students. As we explored in the last chapter, a school's Common Data Set will reveal the average GPA, test scores, and other details about their most recent incoming class, so you can see how your child compares. Consider how the school views the different parts of the application to determine how your child's strengths (and weaknesses) measure up.

Ultimately, you and your child should use this information to narrow the possibilities to a list of *target, reach,* and *safety* schools your child will apply to.

Target schools are schools where your child's academic profile aligns with the profile of the average admitted student. If their test scores and GPA meet or slightly exceed a school's average, that means your child has a reasonable chance of being admitted to that school. Even if your child's GPA and test scores align with a school's profile, but the school is very selective, meaning they admit 10 percent of applicants or less, it's not a true "target school" because of the school's inherent competitiveness. Instead, consider this a reach school.

In general, *reach schools* are schools where your child's profile is slightly below the average admitted student *or* the school is highly selective. Any Ivy or highly selective school should be classified as a reach school even for students with near-perfect scores. Having extraordinary accomplishments in a sport, fine art, or other passion area could boost their chances of admission, putting the school within "reach." Your child should include a couple of reach schools on their application list, but the entire list cannot be exclusively consisting of reach schools. The goal is for your child to be admitted somewhere they will be happy and excel. The worst-case scenario is that your child focuses on reach schools and then fails to be accepted anywhere, it's not common but extremely demoralizing when it does occur. To make sure that doesn't happen, your child should apply to at least one safety school.

Safety schools are schools where your child's GPA, test scores, and other factors are higher than those of the average admitted student, giving your child a high likelihood of admission. It's good for your child to apply to at least one safety school that they would be reasonably happy attending if they don't get into their target or reach schools. That said, if you and your child follow the steps outlined in this book, they should be well-positioned to gain admission to a target school, and maybe even a reach school.

Because Sasha's grades and test scores were near-perfect, most schools on her list, even MIT and Columbia University, looked like target schools. Since these institutions have extremely low admission rates (MIT's 2022 admission rate was 3.96 percent [11] and Columbia University's was 3.73 percent [12]), she treated them as reach schools, and added some more accessible schools to her list. I would advise you and your child to approach their college list the same way.

STEP 5. CONSIDER THE MITIGATING CIRCUMSTANCES

If your child is an American student applying to a public university in a different state, or an international student applying to any US college or university, it's important to be aware of the percentage of students a school typically admits from your state or part of the world. As I mentioned earlier, some US schools, primarily public universities,

---

11   "Class Profile," MIT Admissions, accessed September 4, 2023, https://mitadmissions.org/apply/process/stats/.

12   "Columbia Announces Class of 2026 Admissions Decisions," Columbia University in the City of New York, accessed October 4, 2023, https://www.college.columbia.edu/news/columbia-announces-class-2026-admissions-decisions.

are mandated to admit a certain percentage of students from their state, and thus admit fewer students from outside that state. On the other hand, some schools prioritize a diverse student body and may be more welcoming to out-of-state and foreign students to achieve this goal. Pay special attention to the geographical enrollment profile of students admitted to the schools on your child's list to see if this is likely to increase or decrease their chances of admission.

Sasha had grown up in Malaysia, so it was especially important for her to consider how being an international student might affect her admission chances. There were many public universities on her list, and she was especially interested in the California schools: U.C. Berkeley and U.C. San Diego. Both had 2022 acceptance rates that were higher than MIT and Columbia University—Berkeley's admissions rate was 16.4 percent and UCSD's was a comparatively generous 36 percent.[13,14] On the surface, that makes UC-Berkeley look like a target school and UCSD like a safety school. However, both of those schools are California state universities, required to educate California's children. UC-Berkeley admitted only 5.5 percent of the international students who applied while UCSD admitted a far more generous 18.27 percent.[15]

Other schools, as I mentioned earlier, consider international applicants more favorably. Remember, colleges and universities are communities that value the contributions and perspectives of international students. For example, 10 percent of the freshmen admitted

---

13   "Freshman Admission Profile," UC Berkeley, accessed September 10, 2023, https://admission.universityofcalifornia.edu/campuses-majors/berkeley/freshman-admission-profile.html.

14   "Freshman Admission Summary," UC San Diego, accessed October 4, 2023, https://ir.ucsd.edu/_files/stats-data/admissions/freshmen/ffapadac.pdf.

15   "Student Statistics," UC Berkeley International Office, accessed August 7, 2023, https://internationaloffice.berkeley.edu/sites/default/files/student-stats2022.pdf.

to MIT in 2022 were international students.[16] The bottom line, as always, is research. The more you know about a school, the better you can gauge your child's chances of being admitted.

STEP 6. CONSIDER WHAT ELSE THE SCHOOL MAY BE LOOKING FOR

One little-known strategy to boost your child's chances of admission to a college or university is for them to provide something specific that the school is looking for. No, I'm not talking about a new science building or any sort of big financial investment (beyond the cost of tuition, of course!). I'm talking about schools that have a need for something unique that only your child can provide.

For example, maybe your child is fluent in Farsi and a school is looking to strengthen their Islamic Studies program. Maybe a school wants to grow its grassroots advocacy program, and your student has some significant achievements within this area. Opportunities like these, where your child can fill a school's specific need for a specific type of student, can boost their chances of admission. The only way to know what a school might need is to research that school, looking for places where your child could meet a school's specific need.

In Sasha's case, there were many areas where she could look for this overlap. Her years of work in climate change during high school made her a natural fit for any school on her list that was heavily involved in the fight to save the planet. The fact that she continued to play softball through high school, gaining leadership experience as a captain of the team, provided another differentiator. Not only did she have experience with climate change policy, but she also had the leadership abilities to further her impact. In the end, everything

---

16   "Common Data Set 2020-2021," MIT, accessed October 2, 2023, http://commondata-sets.com/MIT.html.

your student does with passion and focus is something that may add to their college community and may make admissions officers more likely to take notice. Ensure your child's research is thorough enough to determine how they can contribute to the school community.

Declaring an Intended Major as a Differentiator

A school's course catalog can also provide clues as to where your child might best fit in at a specific school. Course catalogs show not only what majors a school offers, but how many students are taking the classes. This is where declaring an *intended major* can be helpful. For example, when Sasha researched majors related to her passion for fighting climate change, there were numerous paths available. By reviewing the course catalogs, she could see which of those majors were already crowded, and which needed more students. If a school had a lot of students majoring in Environmental Sciences, but few in Public Policy, Sasha knew to apply as a Public Policy major with a focus on climate change. In the US, she knew she could switch her major if she decided on it later on. That's one of the benefits of US colleges and universities, they allow you to modify your path as you progress through college.

The Early Decision Decision

Speaking of commitment, one final way your child can boost their chances of admission to a specific school is to apply to that school's "early decision" (ED) deadline. Under ED, a student can apply early in the admissions cycle and receive an admission decision before the regular decision process starts. It's good for schools, allowing them to admit students they know will attend, and good for students, giving them an opportunity to find out the admissions decision sooner, as well as a potential leg up on the competition. But there's a catch. Applying ED is binding. This means that if your student is admitted, they are required to enroll in that school and withdraw all other applications.

Demonstrating commitment to a school by applying ED can be a big advantage for your student. Many schools accept a higher percentage of ED students when compared to regular decision (RD). For example, Cornell University admitted 9 percent of applicants in 2022, but of the students who applied ED, 21 percent were admitted. This holds true with many colleges, but not *all*. Make sure to do the research on the schools your child is considering before committing.

That research should include an understanding of the financial aid process if your family will need assistance paying for college. Use the financial aid calculators required on all college websites to get a (very good) estimate of what your child's tuition will be. A.J. did this when he made his ED decision. His high school record put many top schools in his target range, including several schools in the Ivy League, but at the same time, A.J.'s family made it clear they could not afford the tuition at *any* Ivy. A.J. did his research, and while he applied to a range of top schools, he chose Cornell University for early decision, because (a) Cornell University had a favorable early decision rate *and* (b) was most likely to offer enough financial aid. It turned out to be the right decision. A.J. was accepted and was able to attend Cornell University for five years; he graduated with two degrees without spending a dime on tuition, room and board, or books.

Keep in mind that not all early decision decisions work out *that* well, and may not be for your child, but doing your research really can pay off. Notably, if your child is admitted to a school under ED and the financial award doesn't match your expectations from the Financial Aid Calculator, your child can back out of the otherwise binding contract.

Of course, applying ED is not a guarantee of admission. If your child is not admitted under ED, they will be notified by the ED deadline, which is usually in mid-December. They may be deferred to the RD period, or they may be denied admission entirely. If your child is deferred, their application will be considered with the other RD applicants and should apply to other institutions during RD as well.

If your child isn't comfortable committing to an early decision, some schools offer "early action" (EA). This is like ED in that students apply early and receive their answer early, but different because the decision is non-binding. Additionally, they are still allowed to apply to multiple schools at the same time. Applying EA can also boost your child's chances of admission, but because they aren't making a full commitment, that boost may be smaller than the boost they can get through ED. Some schools, like Stanford University, also offer what's called "restricted early action" (REA), which is still non-binding, but prohibits students from applying to other private colleges during the early part of the cycle.

Phew! Now you know everything you need to know to help your child figure out what schools are right for them and develop their admissions strategy. In the next chapter, we will switch our focus to how your child can "package their passion" by creating an application theme that clearly, concisely, and compellingly presents the story of why they are an ideal fit for their dream school, and why that school's seven-minute decision should be "yes."

CHAPTER 4

AB WORKOUT #2:

APPLICATION THEME

As students, Sam and Libby seemed very similar. They both applied to college with 4.0 GPAs. They both scored 1560 on their SATs. They both wanted to go to school in the US and planned to major in architecture. Libby was accepted to her dream program: USC's B.A. in Architecture. Sam, however, was denied by that very same program.

Why?

What was it about Libby's application that appealed to the admissions officer, whereas Sam's did not?

Sam's application was like a lot of college applications. It indicated that he did well in a wide variety of subjects, and had varied interests: photography, mountain climbing, baseball, and making movies with his friends. He had never taken a class in architecture, but he had taken a trip to Berlin with his parents where he was inspired by his surroundings and rethought his original plan to pursue a business degree. That's what he wrote on the application form when it asked him why he picked architecture as a major.

Libby's application also showed her doing well across a range of subjects, but her elective choices seemed a little more deliberate than Sam's. Her coursework demonstrated a progression from introductory drawing to AP classes in art and design. Outside of the classroom, Libby was the secretary of her school's design and architecture club and spent the summer after her junior year on a Habitat for Humanity project, building houses for the victims of a devastating hurricane. On her application, Libby explained that she chose architecture as a major because her dream was to design and build sustainable, affordable housing. In other words, Libby's application had a *theme* that was clear to anyone reviewing her application.

What's in an App?

College applications have changed a lot since the days when you went to school. Back then, a college application was a lot like a really, really complex job application. You probably filled it out on paper (!), maybe even with a pen (!!), and sent it off in the mail (!!!), which is also the way you probably received your admission decision. Every school had its own, separate application, including separate prompts for separate essays. If you were able to repurpose anything, it was probably your letters of recommendation, and maybe the occasional essay. Other than that, almost everything had to be done from scratch, for every single school you applied to.

Today, that is no longer the case, thanks to technology in general, and more specifically, something called the Common Application (aka the "Common App").[17] If you haven't experienced the Common App yet, you'll discover it's a genius invention. Rather than filling out a

---

17   "About," Common App, accessed October 04, 2023, https://www.commonapp.org/about.

unique application for every single school your child applies to, the Common App allows them to complete one basic, online application (including their personal statement) and, with minor supplements, submit it to many (or even all) of the schools they are applying to at the same time. Over 1,000 colleges and universities in all fifty US states and twenty countries utilize the service, including most of the institutions you've heard of. It's not a question of who accepts the Common App, but rather who *doesn't*.

Technological advances like the Common App have made some aspects of applying to college much easier, like ensuring transcripts and test score reports reach their intended recipients. However, the overall process has probably gotten more difficult since you went to school. Why? Now that it's one centralized process, schools can request even more material from applicants. Instead of the job-application-style form plus an essay or two you may have submitted, today's college applications are more like a "packet" containing:

- application form including your child's contact information, personal data, and a basic overview of their educational history;
- transcript;
- standardized test scores;
- essays;
- letters of recommendation; and
- other materials which may be necessary for a specific school or specific course of study, including:
- artistic portfolios (visual art, writing, music, dance, etc.),
- performance videos for theater, music, or athletic programs,

- writing samples, and

- supplementary essays.

In addition, some institutions recommend including a resumé organizing the applicant's achievements, extracurricular activities, and work experience. If the school held an interview with your child as part of the application process, the interviewer's impressions will also be considered.

It's a lot of information for an admissions officer to process, whether they take seven minutes or a leisurely fifteen to make their decision about your child. With so much information to wade through, an application theme can help an admission officer quickly get a sense of your child.

That's what this chapter is all about.

What's an Application Theme?

An application theme doesn't need to be anything super-creative or complicated—it's just a unifying thread that ties all the different elements of your child's application together. It helps your child tell the story of who they are, how they have spent their time in and out of high school, what matters most to them, and what they are looking for in a college experience. They can find inspiration for their theme anywhere in their life. Some choose to use an aspect of their identity, heritage, or values, while others focus on a memorable experience (good or bad), or a lifelong dream. The only real requirement, at least in my view, is that your child's application theme ties into their passion. In fact, one simple, almost-foolproof, way to look at an application theme is as the story of your child's passion. Explore where the passion came from, how it developed, what they have learned from it (especially about themselves), and where they hope their passion will take them in the future. *Frankly, this is a good start to a "personal statement" essay right there, so we'll put a pin in it and come back to it later.*

The purpose of the application theme is to make sure your child's application clearly demonstrates who your student is as a person. This makes it easier to see why your child would be a good fit in the community the admissions officer is trying to build. By highlighting specific strengths and experiences, a theme can even illustrate how your child embodies a school's mission or values, which could further help differentiate them from the other applicants.

Application themes work because they take what might otherwise appear to be a collection of random facts about your child and tie everything together. The theme tells a story that gives your child's experiences context and meaning. Of course, whatever theme your child chooses should be accurate and reflect who your child really is, not who you think a specific school wants them to be. Ideally, your child's application theme will showcase the best version of who they are, from their past accomplishments to their future potential.

DEVELOPING AN APPLICATION THEME

Like many things in this book, you and your child should start thinking about their application theme right around when they start high school. That doesn't mean there is a lot of actual work to do in this area at that point, but rather it helps your student start high school with the right mindset. To be accepted to a top US school, your student needs to approach high school with intention. Like Libby, they need to use those four years to discover and develop their passions, as

AN APPLICATION THEME SHOULD DEMONSTRATE COMMITMENT, FOCUS AND GROWTH—ALL THINGS ADMISSIONS OFFICERS WILL BE LOOKING FOR.

opposed to following Sam's example and exploring a lot of random activities and options with no real plan. An application theme should demonstrate commitment, focus, and growth. Admissions officers look for these personal qualities in every application and the application theme will only help emphasize your child's unique characteristics.

Until your child starts the actual college application process, the application theme is simply something you both need to keep in mind as they select their classes and pursue extracurricular activities. Their theme may evolve and change over the course of high school, and that's normal. This evolution will eventually be part of the story your child tells prospective schools. Every college application tells a story, whether intentionally or accidentally. The goal is for your student to take control of their story from the start of high school, making choices that will demonstrate a pattern of growth and commitment that sets them apart from their fellow applicants.

The application theme is an effective tool because it gives your child's story clarity and brings it to life. In those few minutes an admissions officer spends reviewing their application, you want them to get the most accurate picture possible of who your child is and why they are a good fit for that specific school. An application theme should enable an admissions officer to quickly understand what matters to your child, what they excel at, and what they may be like as a student. This makes the admissions officer feel like they "know" the student they are admitting. Each element of the application plays a part in painting that picture and reinforcing the message that they're making the right decision in accepting your student into their next class.

Let's go through each element of a college application step by step to demonstrate how the application theme pulls everything together.

THE APPLICATION FORM

The application form is where the admissions officer will first meet your student. It shows a basic overview of their high school experience and goals for the future. Specifically, the Common App includes the following sections:

- applicant info;

- future plans (intended major and interests);

- demographics;

- family information;

- education (where they went to school and when);

- academics (their courses and grades);

- extracurricular activities and work experience; and

- teacher and school evaluations.

Other college applications are like the Common App, so this is a good overview of what to expect from any school your child might apply to.

If you look at the actual Common App form, you might get the impression that there is little space for your child to develop their theme. The reality is, those first, introductory pages are where your child's application theme will first be established...if they have one.

For example, you'll see that the second segment on the form, right after your child's contact information, is titled "Future Plans." Not their grades, what classes they took, or their extracurricular activities. Admission officers want to know, right away, what your child hopes to learn during their time in college. From that moment on, the admissions officer will be viewing the information on your child's application through that lens. Do their choices like class selection and extracurricular activities indicate a passion and aptitude to bring those plans to life? This is one reason why applying undeclared, especially without any demonstration of a strong passion or area of interest, can be a huge strike against your student. It makes them look like they haven't given their future much thought. Of course, it isn't much better for your child to declare an area of interest but have nothing else on their application form indicating that their interest is genuine.

That may have been Sam's problem. While he did well in his classes and was active in a lot of extracurricular activities, without any evidence of a thought-out theme, the only story they told was of a student who tried a lot of things but didn't necessarily commit to any of them. Libby's story, on the other hand, instantly established she had discovered she had a passion for architecture, explored various aspects of the field during high school, and viewed studying it in college as a natural next step toward a life doing something she loved.

Which story seems more compelling to you?

Since the application form is the first thing an admissions officer sees, your child must use it to establish their theme from the beginning. This isn't the only (or even best) place for their theme to come alive, however. Essays, extracurricular activities, and letters of recommendation all provide an opportunity to go deeper into the theme.

On that note, keep in mind that the application form has limited space to list activities, honors, and awards, so many high-achieving students find there is not enough room to list everything of significance that they have done. If your student has this problem, they should first enter the experiences that are most relevant to their application theme. Look at the application form as a place to feature the highlights of your child's story and begin to develop the theme, almost like a teaser of the details to come. There will be room to address more of your child's accomplishments and experiences in other areas of the application.

TRANSCRIPTS

How can a transcript, which is just a list of the classes your child took and how well they did in those classes, support a theme? By indicating (a) your child took the right classes to prepare them to succeed in their area of interest, (b) their course load was appropriately rigorous, and (c) they succeeded in learning the material. Sam's course selection told a story that he did well in his classes but did not choose his classes with intention. Libby's choice of classes indicated a strong interest in architecture *and* success in high-level classes relevant to the field, which supported her theme. All else being equal, this difference made Libby a more attractive candidate for admission than Sam.

STANDARDIZED TEST SCORES

This is an area where your student really doesn't have much control, other than preparing to the point where they have strong scores across the board. It helps test scores to be high in the area closest to their intended major, which will give more support to their theme. That means strong English scores for humanities majors and strong math scores for STEM students, but recall that most highly selective institutions are admitting students with very high scores across the board.

If your student is applying to a test-optional school and can avoid posting a low score, especially one that directly relates to their application theme, that is probably the way to go. Conversely, strong standardized test scores can be posted to highlight their strengths in areas related to their application theme.

ESSAYS

Essays are your child's best opportunity to highlight and explain their application theme. You'd be surprised how many students get thrown off by a prompt and fail to use their essays to make a bigger statement about who they are and who they will become. Some students simply answer the question posed without thinking strategically about what they are saying and the impact it can have on an admissions officer. They don't consider the larger story they're trying to tell.

I make sure my students never make that mistake.

We'll get deeper into how to write an effective college essay later, but since this chapter is about application theme, I will state the obvious: whatever your child writes about, whatever the prompt might be, they should find a way to connect it back to their theme.

The personal statement is a perfect opportunity for your child to tell their story and describe the overall theme of their college application, including:

- Who they are as a person.

- What they are passionate about.

- What they hope to learn at college.

- What they can bring to the college community.

You'll notice that these points directly align with the essay format I suggested earlier in this chapter.

In addition to the personal essay, your child will probably be asked to respond to several school-specific prompts. If they get to choose between a few different prompts, they should select the prompt that presents the best opportunity for them to illustrate another aspect of their theme. If they're drawn to a topic that doesn't really relate to their theme and they can't find some way to tie it back to the bigger picture, they should choose a different topic or prompt altogether. At the same time, your child must avoid choosing topics or prompts that lead them to tell the same story multiple times. Each essay is a unique opportunity to highlight a different aspect of your child's overall theme and each chance must be used wisely.

To get an idea of how this works in real life, let's look at a few common essay prompts and think about how our future architects, Sam and Libby, might use them to make their case.

Here is a common prompt: *Share an experience that has sparked your curiosity or intellectual passion and how it has influenced your academic or career goals.* Both Sam and Libby might use a prompt like that as a springboard to talk about their first experience with architecture, like Sam's trip to Berlin or Libby's work with Habitat for Humanity, and how it inspired them.

For a subsequent essay, Libby could answer the following prompt: *Discuss a community service project or activity that has been meaningful to you and how it has impacted your perspective on the world.* Here, she could further discuss her experiences with Habitat for Humanity and how it inspired her dream of building new affordable housing solutions for needy families. Alternatively, Libby could further explore her experience with Habitat for Humanity in a different way by answering this prompt: *Discuss a time when you collaborated with others to achieve a common goal and what you learned from the experience.* She could answer this prompt by describing what she learned from working with others, her own contributions, and possibly how she grew her leadership skills.

Sticking with the application theme is closely tied to the overall strategy aspect of writing college essays, which we will get to later in this book. Choose prompts that will give your student the best opportunity to showcase their theme and their story. The more they reinforce the theme, the clearer the picture of who they are will emerge making it even easier for an admissions officer to get inspired to say "yes."

LETTERS OF RECOMMENDATION

After your child's application essays, recommendation letters are the next best place to reinforce their application theme. The key is to ensure the recommenders also focus on the application theme while providing authority and authentication of your child's story. This isn't always easy to do. I will cover how to choose the right recommender and then guide them appropriately in a later chapter. For now, I want to concentrate on how your child can use letters of recommendation specifically to reinforce their application theme.

First, your child should choose at least one recommender who is connected to their theme. This may be in the form of an "additional recommendation" because it's usually required that teacher recommendations come from individuals with an affiliation with your child's high school. Your chosen recommender should be closely connected to your child's passion and understand its importance in their life. In Libby's case, a good recommender might be the adult who supervised her Habitat for Humanity project, especially if she did well there. An adult who knows your child well and can speak to the aspects of their story that are most important to their application theme should be at the top of your child's list when it comes time to request letters of recommendation.

Once your child chooses their recommenders (and those recommenders agree to write them a strong endorsement), ensure your child discusses their theme and ask them to write their recommendation with that theme in mind. This is a great way to ensure these letters of recommendation are effective in supporting your child's candidacy.

INTERVIEWS

Not all colleges require interviews, but most top schools at least offer them, whether they are conducted in person on campus, virtually in a chat room, or at a meeting site with a local alumnus or representative. Interviews can be stressful and may feel like they're out of your child's "wheelhouse," especially if they have never interviewed for a job or admission to a private school or selective program before. However, even if your child's dream school offers "optional" interviews, I recommend they find a way to sit down with someone, either virtually or in person, and have a conversation about who they are and their future plans. A college interview is an excellent opportunity for your child to reinforce their application theme and demonstrate their serious interest in the school.

As scary as the prospect of a conversation with a strange adult (during which they will be evaluated!) might seem to your child, an interview with a representative of a school they hope to attend has very little downside. It's the only opportunity during the application process for your child to show off the real, genuine human being they are, share their story, and respond to follow-up questions in real time.

With a little preparation, your child should do just fine.

Once your child has scheduled an interview, they should spend some time thinking about their application theme and some of the stories and experiences that best illustrate it. Help them remember some of the experiences that have shaped their choices and led them to where they are.

They should practice answering some common interview questions and telling their story. This is especially important for non-native English speakers. An interview is an opportunity for your child to demonstrate that they will be comfortable attending an American school where they will likely be communicating and learning in English.

Regardless of where in the world they are coming from, your child should prepare to share some specific examples of how they have embodied their application theme in their life and actions. They should demonstrate their passion and enthusiasm by discussing why their theme matters to them and how it has influenced their choices and goals for the future. If there is a way to connect this back to their interviewer in some way, like a shared passion or interest, that's even better.

IT'S A CHANCE FOR YOUR CHILD TO BRING THEIR APPLICATION THEME TO LIFE, TO TALK ABOUT THEIR PASSION WITH PASSION.

That might sound like a challenge, and it very well may be. Not all young people are comfortable talking with adults one on one, especially strangers, and your child may worry about stumbling or saying something "wrong," especially if English is not their first language. College interviewers don't expect perfection, but they do expect an honest, open conversation that will give them a window into who your child is and how they might fit into their school. It's a chance for your child to bring their application theme to life, to talk about their passion *with* passion, and to demonstrate exactly why an admissions officer should get excited about the prospect of having them as a student.

Next Steps

Start talking with your child about their passions, interests, and possible future course of study. Make a list of potential application themes that can be developed from those areas. Encourage your child to think about the story they want to share about themselves both as a student and a human being. What experiences do they want to highlight? Finally, whether your child is a freshman or further along in their high school career, guide them toward choosing classes and extracurricular activities that will engage their passions and relate to their theme. We'll take a closer look at those choices in the next two chapters, beginning with role of extracurricular activities in the application.

CHAPTER 5

AB WORKOUT #3:

EXTRACURRICULAR ACTIVITIES

Have you ever heard the saying, "All work and no play makes Jack a dull boy?" Well, it turns out all work and no play can also keep Jack from getting into his dream school as we learned when we met poor Alan, who didn't get into Yale, earlier in this book.

I've already pointed out that top US colleges and universities aren't looking for study machines, who only see the light of day when they walk from the classroom to the library. The best schools in America want students who are well-rounded human beings with full lives, dreams, and goals that go beyond getting a 1600 on their SAT. That means the things your child pursues outside of school aren't just "for fun." These activities are a necessary element of a successful high school career, developing personal qualities in your child that classes, tests, and homework just can't.

Because they are so important to the overall story your child is trying to tell, their extracurricular activities need to be chosen and pursued with both intention and enjoyment. Your child's extracurriculars are what will set them apart from all the other kids with similar grades and standardized test scores by showing who they are as a human being. In this chapter, we'll take a closer look at all things extracurricular, and how to use your child's time outside of high school to help prepare them for admission to their dream school.

What Counts as an Extracurricular Activity?

Technically, almost anything your child does regularly for no academic credit is an extracurricular activity. They should gain something from the experience, so watching TV and playing video games every night does not count. However, if your child writes a weekly blog recapping their favorite TV shows, or launches and runs a video game review website, that's an example of taking their passion and turning it into a viable extracurricular activity. If your child is learning and developing skills, anything from an afterschool job at a fast-food joint to running a marathon to volunteering weekly at a soup kitchen qualifies.

Of course, some extracurricular activities are still "better" than others. But maybe not in the way you think.

Whether your child chooses extracurricular activities that are athletic, creative, professional, educational, service-based or anything else, they must give your child an opportunity to demonstrate commitment, passion, and leadership. The level at which your child participates (the "depth of commitment") matters more than the activity type itself. Demonstrating greatness in the extracurricular will make admissions officers pay attention—consider an Olympic gymnast versus a member of the JV football team. While we can't all be Olympians, we can all try to leave a legacy within the community of our chosen activity.

In the college admissions world, there are four basic tiers of extra-curricular activities:

TIER FOUR

Tier Four activities are those common activities I mentioned above, like playing on a school team, working a part-time job, playing a musical instrument in a band or on their own, being a member of a club, or doing volunteer work. These are things anyone can do, so they are not regarded as particularly special, although they are better than nothing. Tier Four activities at least offer a window into the sorts of things your child is interested in outside of school, especially if they are centered on your child's passions. If your child really digs in and focuses on a few key passions throughout high school, they should be able to raise the bar enough to participate in some Tier Three activities.

TIER THREE

Tier Three extracurricular activities demonstrate more passion, commitment, and a higher skill level than Tier Four. They include more academics-based clubs and organizations like Model UN or the Robotics Team, clubs that advocate for social change, anything that requires a deeper level of immersion and commitment to participate. If your child earns more responsibility on the job, that raises them to Tier Three. Similarly, if your child plays a sport and earns a spot on a selective club team, or is named player of the week on their high school team, again, because they are demonstrating a higher level of passion, commitment, and skill that bumps them up to Tier Three.

When your child sticks with something they care about, growing their skill and knowledge, they can elevate themselves above other applicants. If that skill continues to develop and your child continues to gain valuable experience, they may find themselves involved in some Tier Two activities.

TIER TWO

Tier Two extracurricular activities aren't things your child can just sign up for. They're common and accessible to many students, but they're generally earned or elected positions, like leadership roles or starting positions on competitive sports teams, often after years spent dedicated to pursuing their passion. Not every student who tries to reach Tier Two gets there; reaching this level requires a high degree of commitment and dedication to their passion, as well as, in many cases, actual talent for whatever they are doing. That's what it takes to be selected for an All-State football team, win a prestigious regional debate competition, or be elected to a leadership position at the school district or regional level—all Tier Two-level accomplishments.

It's not easy to reach Tier Two, but that's the point. If your child chooses their extracurricular activities with intention and devotes themselves to one passion above all others, it significantly ups their chances of getting there, differentiating themselves from their peers. If they're incredibly successful, they may even make it to Tier One.

TIER ONE

Tier One extracurricular activities are where you find the unicorns: the Olympic athletes, national competition winners, successful inventors, published authors, and other students so accomplished, an admissions officer probably only meets a few of them each year (at an Ivy) or even spread across an entire career (at a less-selective school). There are Tier One activities to match every passion, including athletics, arts, science, leadership, and even service. Ultimately, very few students will achieve this level. With a few exceptions, like being selected for a prestigious summer program that admits multiple students (more on that in a moment), the students who get to Tier One are often standing up there alone. There can only be one winner of a competition, one head of a national organization, one creator of a singular piece of art or technology. For that reason, students who reach Tier One tend to have top schools fighting over them, instead of having to prove themselves to get in.

Jumping Tiers

If you just read that last segment and thought, "Getting into a prestigious summer program sounds a lot easier than winning a national competition," you would be right. While your child can continue pursuing their normal extracurriculars (athletics, debate, etc.), the longer summer break is a great opportunity for your child to take their passion to the Tier Two level.

If your child is planning to apply to a top college in the US, a summer program is something you and your child should consider exploring. Students from the US certainly will be taking advantage of these opportunities. The more important reason to consider these programs, however, is because of what they can do for your child. The best way for a student to take their passion to the next level is spending several weeks dedicated to that passion and nothing else.

Finding the right summer program is as simple as Googling your child's passion and the words "summer program." Whatever your child is interested in, there is a program available to provide exposure and growth in the area. Students can live in foreign countries to learn a new language and culture, do research projects on a college campus, volunteer, engage with the fine arts through a theater or dance troupe…the list is almost endless.

Participating in one (or more) of these programs is generally an automatic upgrade to Tier Two for that extracurricular activity since it demonstrates a high level of commitment, curiosity, and passion. The application and acceptance process, especially for the more selective, college-based programs, is an accomplishment on its own. There are additional tangible benefits during the college admissions process these programs offer your child, such as:

- Creating a work product that can be submitted for honors and awards.

- Earning college credit from prestigious schools.

- Gaining an admissions advantage at programs that are affiliated with a college or university (*if there is a summer program affiliated with your child's dream school, put down this book and figure out how to get them an application NOW!*).

- Recruiting (*College representatives often attend performances and view portfolios or research and will recruit students who make an impression*).

- Submitting a "warm-up" application before they do the real thing when applying to college.

Depending on where you are in the world and your family's financial situation, it may not be possible for your child to participate in a summer program. But if there is any way to make it happen, including sponsorships and GoFundMe campaigns, I highly encourage it. This is the most effective way to turn your child's passion into a strong differentiating factor in their candidacy for their dream school.

How Does it All Look on Paper?

Again, all this information needs to be absorbed and evaluated by an admissions officer in about seven minutes. How does an admissions officer process it all? The Extracurricular Profile within the Common Application offers the most succinct overview of a student's passion, commitment, and growth. From there, the admission officer will have a good sense of which "tier" the student's activities typically fall within.

A student who has no extracurricular activities, or only a couple of Tier Four experiences, would be classified as having a "weak" extracurricular profile. Students like this are usually rejected by top US schools. I'm confident your student will not be one of those, so we can safely move to the next level.

Most students have what admissions officers call a "standard" extracurricular profile. These are students who pursue multiple activities, but none at an especially high level. Being "well-rounded" sounds like a good thing, and it is in theory, but there is such a thing as *too* well-rounded. This is especially true if your student doesn't participate in any activities at a high level—how passionate can they really be about something if they've failed to demonstrate any growth at all?

Instead of listing a bunch of Tier Four and Tier Three activities, your child should aim to concentrate their efforts, devoting more time to no more than two or three real passions. This would give them what admissions officers call a "solid" extracurricular profile. Solid profiles show tangible achievements in the areas where your child is passionate, and upward movement between tiers.

If your child can reach Tier Two in an area where they are passionate, their extracurricular profile will rise from "solid" to "strong." Strong extracurricular profiles are often called "contrast profiles," where a student reaches Tier Two in two areas of interest—sometimes that are related to each other. Think about a star athlete who also writes about sports for their school newspaper or a volunteer coordinator who spent the summer at a youth climate summit. You don't want your child to aim for greatness in too many extracurriculars, they need the time and space to be able to focus. However, having two or three areas of passion, as opposed to just one, gives your child's extracurricular profile depth.

Extracurriculars, Year by Year

As I mentioned earlier in the chapter, the best way to make sure your child is getting the most out of their extracurricular activities is to choose them with intention. That means thinking through what your child is doing and why, and visualizing where it might take them as they progress through high school. Top schools expect your child's high school years to be about discovering and developing their passions. Ideally, what should they be accomplishing when?

FRESHMAN YEAR

Your child should be entering high school with an idea of what they want to do. Still, if there is ever a good time to try a lot of things, freshman year is that time. If your child wants to play three sports, raise money for the unhoused, and compete in the Science Decathlon, let them go for it. Now is the time for them to explore and figure out what they're good at, what they love to do, and where they can see possibilities for the future.

SOPHOMORE YEAR

Now that your child has had their fun, it's time to get serious. Your child should cut out any activity that is not meaningful to them and try to limit the ones they continue with to two or three, ideally in three different areas, like the arts, sports, and service or robotics, drama, and choir. (And sports, but we'll get to that later.) You want them to think ahead: what kind of leadership or achievement opportunities will be possible in the future? If your child is not a natural leader or their activity is a solo one, they should think about what they will do with that activity to demonstrate growth. Look for activities your child (a) loves to do, and (b) does well. This sweet spot enables your child to rise to Tier Two.

JUNIOR YEAR

Now is the time for your child to seek out those leadership opportunities they've been planning for. Yes, I did say colleges need a mix of leaders and followers, but when it comes to admissions, top schools *really* like leaders. If your child has chosen an activity that they are truly passionate about, after two years, they should be able to attain a position of responsibility. Ensure your child is aware of this as they progress so they can look for opportunities to get further involved, allowing for improvement and growth. This could look like expanding their organization, creating a better product, or earning more honors and awards. The goal is to aim for excellence in whatever they do. In this process, excellence gets noticed.

SENIOR YEAR

This is when students cap off their extracurricular activities with their "crowning achievements." They should hold leadership positions whenever they can, apply for honors and awards when possible, and put in that final push to get the most out of their passions before they move on to college. The first few months of senior year generally matter the most because students can report those activities on their Common Application. Keep in mind, earning an award later in the year is still a good thing and can be reported to admissions officers in the form of an update.

Everybody Plays (or at least, everybody should)

I've been talking a lot about how your child should not pursue too many passions during high school, instead concentrating on the two to three things that they love and are best at. There is one notable exception to this rule, and that exception is extracurricular athletics.

This brings me back to Alan, who gave up playing sports to concentrate on academics. Was Alan rejected *because* he stopped playing sports? Probably not. However, what I can say with reasonable certainty is that because of their numerous social and physical benefits, playing a sport is almost always preferable to not playing one. I recommend you and your child find a way to make at least one sport a regular part of their life.

SPORTS MATTER

Just how important are sports at top US colleges and universities? There's one easy way to find the answer... by following the money. The average salary of a college professor in the USA is just a hair under $100,000.[18] Wondering how much the highest paid college athletics coach makes? During the 2020/2021 school year, Duke

---

18 "Professor Salaries," Indeed, accessed October 04, 2023, https://www.indeed.com/career/professor/salaries.

University paid their basketball coach a mind-boggling $13,700,000.[19] Contrast that salary with that of the school's president, Vincent Price, who earned a comparatively paltry $1,500,000 in 2019.[20]

Athletics are different from other extracurricular activities like choir or drama or the ecology club. They teach students about almost everything that matters in life: teamwork and collaboration, leadership and responsibility, perseverance and resilience, time management and organization, respect and sportsmanship. No wonder, according to a study by the Aspen Institute, nearly 90 percent of CEOs surveyed played a sport in high school. In another study limited to female C-suite members, that number jumps to a whopping 96 percent![21] That may not prove playing a sport is the key to success, but it certainly qualifies as a strong indicator.

ONE COMMON MYTH ABOUT SPORTS IS THAT THEY ONLY MATTER IF YOU'RE GOOD AT THEM.

One common myth about sports is that they only matter if you're good at them. In fact, you can be passionate about sports and be a terrible player. Not only do

---

19 Derek Saul, "Duke Paid Krzyzewski $13.7 Million In 2020-21, Record Compensation For A College Coach," Forbes, May 17, 2022, https://www.forbes.com/sites/dereksaul/2022/05/17/duke-paid-krzyzewski-137-million-in-2020-21-record-compensation-for-a-college-coach/?sh=6363bc841340.

20 Chris Kuo, "Revealed: Who made how much at Duke in 2020-21," The Duke Chronicle, November 15, 2021, https://www.dukechronicle.com/article/2021/11/coach-k-salary-duke-university-administrator-salaries-vincent-price-president-executive.

21 Lauren Thomas, "Want to Be a CEO Later? Play Sports Now," CNBC, January 11, 2017, https://www.cnbc.com/2017/01/11/want-to-be-a-ceo-later-play-sports-now.html.

sports teach all the things I listed above and more, but there are also plenty of career opportunities in sports for people who aren't even good enough to make the varsity squad in high school. Careers in statistics, marketing, training, journalism, and management all exist in the world of sports…if your child loves anything sports-related, there are endless ways to leverage whatever skills they do have to build a future that's at least tangentially related. Since most colleges have sports teams, they offer plenty of places for your student to start. So, don't tell your child to quit the baseball team just because they can't hit a curveball. They may be able to write a Pulitzer Prize-winning article on baseball or recruit a top pitcher to their favorite team.

You never know.

On the other hand, sometimes you *do* know. Maybe you're the parent of a student-athlete who, from an early age, has been the MVP of every team they've ever been on or taken home more medals and trophies than you have space for. If you're the parent of a child like that, who could conceivably play college sports and has the desire to do it, we'll take a deep dive into the athletic recruitment process later in this book.

Next Steps

Whatever grade your child is in right now, talk with them about their passions and which extracurriculars best support those passions. Think about what your child is currently doing, where continued participation might lead, and begin putting together a plan with some possible goals to aim for during their remaining high school years. Finally, if your child can participate, identify some summer programs that will help them take their passion to the next level.

In the next chapter, we'll look at how your child's course selection can prepare them for success on their college applications…or not.

AB WORKOUT #4:

COURSE SELECTION

Back when you went to school, you might not have given much thought to your course selection, or, more specifically, to what this said about you. You took the core classes required to graduate and if you were college-minded, you probably took those classes at the Honors level, or, if your school offered it, the Advanced Placement level. You probably concentrated on classes in subjects you liked, went as far as you could (or felt like going) in those areas where you were academically strong, and used your electives to relax and have fun, or pursue a passion like drama, music, or art. If those classes were sending any kind of message to college admissions officers about what kind of student you would be, it was more likely through your grades than the actual classes. All that mattered was that you did well and met the college's requirements.

Today, as you've probably already gathered from this book, college admission is more complicated now. In a world where more students have a 4.0 GPA (or higher), admissions officers at top US schools look at applicants' transcripts for clues as to how hard they worked to earn that 4.0, what they focused on during high school, and a peek into who they are as people. To do all that and impress admissions officers, your child's courses should align with their application theme and intended major, challenge them academically, further their passions, and be taught by top teachers. We will now break this down, section by section.

COURSES MUST ALIGN WITH APPLICATION THEME AND INTENDED MAJOR

Remember Sam and Libby, the two architecture majors we met a few chapters back? Sam took a wide range of courses in high school and did well in all of them, but nothing he did was specifically supportive of a major in architecture. His course selection painted a picture of someone who was unfocused. Libby's choices were more specific, taking several classes she would need as an architecture major, including two AP courses that not only proved she could compete in that major at the college level, but gave her actual college credit (more on AP classes in a moment). No offense to Sam, but you want your child to be more like Libby in this area.

COURSES MUST BE ACADEMICALLY CHALLENGING

Top colleges don't admit a lot of students who coast through high school, unless that student is one of the few with a solid Tier One accomplishment on their record and have coasted through everything else. Admissions officers are looking for applicants who actively seek out opportunities to learn and challenge themselves academically. This means your child needs to push themselves in the classroom. The goal is to find that sweet spot where they take the most challenging classes they can handle, ideally with the highest-level classes supporting one of their passions. This includes honors classes, Advanced Placement classes, and the International Baccalaureate program, which we will cover in depth in a moment.

There are, of course, some caveats here. If your child is pursuing a primarily creative or athletic college path as opposed to an academic one, their course load can be less rigorous, because they're using their energy to excel in other areas. You also don't want your child to over-extend themselves and, by trying to be great at everything, wind up great at nothing. You and your student should be realistic about the amount of work they can handle and focus their highest efforts on the courses that are most closely aligned with their passions.

COURSES SHOULD FOCUS ON TOPICS ALIGNING WITH STUDENT'S PASSION

Admissions officers will be looking for evidence that your student has a passion, gained knowledge and experience in this area, and prepared themselves for what they want to study. That was another key difference between Sam and Libby's applications. While Sam may have really loved architecture, nothing about his course selection indicated this. Libby's, however, revealed a passion for art and design with a high level of preparation to demonstrate that commitment.

COURSES SHOULD BE TAUGHT BY TOP TEACHERS

This matters more than you might think, as evidenced by this crazy-but-true story. I knew a student, Krista, who signed up for AP Art History at her high school. She was passionate about art and design and was considering an art-related major and career. She was excited to learn more about the origins of art. Instead, she learned next to nothing. While Krista hoped to learn about the use of light in Renaissance art or the origins of the Modernist movement, her teacher used the class period to show his students movies. Specifically, American musicals from the 1930s. *Swing Time* was a favorite...look it up!

If this teacher's students were going to learn what they needed to know to pass the AP Art History exam, they had to study it on their own. Krista didn't realize this until it was too late. She got a two out of possible five on the AP test. Essentially, she failed.

Granted, most *bad* teachers aren't as negligent as Krista's was, but some educators are definitely better than others. Your child should seek out teachers who have a good reputation, who will challenge them, and take a genuine interest in their progress. In a perfect world, your child's teachers will want to partner with them as they work to reach their educational goals. Look at your child's teachers as a support team, with each person playing their part in getting your child ready for the challenges to come. Do what you can to learn about the teachers at your child's school by asking other parents, talking with your child, and researching online to ensure your child's team is a team of All-Stars.

Working With Your Child's Counselor

If your child's high school teachers are a team, their counselor is the team captain. Try to develop a strong working relationship with their counselor from the get-go as it can give them a huge leg up when it comes to planning their whole high school career (including course selection) and applying to college. Most counselors want to be helpful but won't know how to help your student until they reach out and ask for guidance. Do what you can to help your student get comfortable talking with adults and forming strong working relationships so they can benefit from the help school counselors can provide.

It's best to reach out to their counselor early in your child's freshman year, if not the summer before high school begins. Schedule a meeting with the counselor to discuss your child's academic goals, their passions and interests, and any concerns you may have. Be sure to emphasize your child's college aspirations and the importance of selecting the right courses to meet those goals. Since your child will still be very much a child, don't expect them to have a crystal-clear vision of their future just yet (although they might!). The idea is to give the counselor a sense of who your child is and what matters to them, so the counselor can guide them toward the appropriate classes to get them where they want to go.

Nurture the relationship with your child's counselor throughout their high school years. The counselor can guide your child toward the right opportunities as their interests evolve. Keep your child on track to meet the school's graduation requirements, and, if your student attends school in the US, they should have some familiarity with requirements for college admission at various schools in your state and region, along with a selection of bigger name universities across the country.

Different counselors have varying degrees of knowledge. A weaker counselor might only be familiar with a selection of schools in the state, while a good counselor who knows your child should be able to suggest a range of schools across the US that are a good fit for them. Once they know your child's target schools, they can ensure your child will meet any prerequisites at these institutions. Most colleges and universities have specific prerequisites for admission, like a certain number of years of math, science, or foreign language classes, so work with the counselor to be sure your child is taking the courses they need. The counselor should also know (or be able to quickly look up) any college's minimum standardized test scores and GPA.

A good counselor will work with you and your child proactively to guide them through high school and admission to the right college. They have an incentive: the more students they help get accepted to great colleges, the better their school's reputation. Unfortunately, not everyone cares about being great at their job, so if your child's counselor is not meeting their needs, you may need to look elsewhere for support and advice. This could include your child's favorite teachers or professional college counselors.

Advanced Placement or International Baccalaureate?

As I mentioned earlier, the high school students with the strongest academic records are those who veer off the standard (or once-standard) course of honors classes and challenge themselves with either Advanced Placement (AP) classes or an International Baccalaureate (IB) degree. Both are extremely rigorous academic programs designed to challenge high school students with college-level coursework, further developing their critical thinking skills. Both can receive college credit depending on the institution. The two programs vary in several ways.

Advanced Placement courses are a product of the College Board and are found in most high schools in the US and around the world. International Baccalaureate was founded in Geneva, Switzerland, and represents more of a "classical" education. The IB program historically has resulted in a diploma as opposed to singular courses taken separately from one another as is common within AP programs. Both pathways offer your child an opportunity to study core subjects and electives at the highest possible level for a high school student, which is especially beneficial if some of those subjects align with your student's passions. We'll look at these two options one at a time, beginning with the AP program.

ADVANCED PLACEMENT

The Advanced Placement program is a set of courses and corresponding exams developed by the College Board, the non-profit, US-based educational organization that also produces the SAT. AP courses are specifically designed to provide high school students with college-level academic coursework and students who take AP courses have the opportunity to earn college credit, advanced placement in college (hence the name), or, in some cases, both.

The AP program offers courses in a wide range of subjects, including English, math, science, social studies, and several of the most common foreign (non-English) languages, plus Latin. The courses are taught at a higher level than typical high school courses because they try to mimic college-level courses, covering more material and requiring more work from students. At the end of the course, students take a standardized exam scored on a scale of one to five. Colleges and universities often grant credit or advanced placement to students who score a three or higher on an AP exam, depending on the institution's policy and the specific AP course.

As of this writing and according to the College Board website, AP is offering the following forty courses:

African Diaspora	Latin
Art and Design	Macroeconomics
Biology	Microeconomics
Calculus AB	Music Theory
Calculus BC	Physics 1: Algebra-Based
Chemistry	Physics 2: Algebra-Based
Chinese Language and Culture	Physics C: Electricity and Magnetism
Comparative Government and Politics	Physics C: Mechanics
Computer Science A	Precalculus
Computer Science Principles	Psychology
Economics (Micro and Macro)	Research
English Language and Composition	Seminar
English Literature and Composition	Spanish Language and Culture
Environmental Science	Spanish Literature and Culture
European History	Statistics

French Language and Culture	Studio Art: 2-D Design
German Language and Culture	Studio Art: 3-D Design
Human Geography	Studio Art: Drawing
Italian Language and Culture	United States Government and Politics
Japanese Language and Culture	United States History

You'll notice from this list that the AP system offers opportunities for your child to do college-level work in multiple areas, so there's a good chance your child can find some AP courses that support their passion and help prepare them for even deeper learning in college.

The courses do change occasionally, but the more likely issue is that your child's high school may not offer all the available courses. Just because your child's school doesn't offer a particular class they want to take, doesn't mean they can't take the course. If an AP class is not available through your child's high school, let your child's counselor know. They may be able to arrange for your student to take the class outside of school. If the counselor is not helpful, you can explore other options:

- *Find another, local high school that offers the course.* Often schools will grant approval for your student to take the course at this other school.

- *Arrange for your child to take the course online.* The College Board has their own AP Classroom program with online educators offering courses covering the AP test material. Some programs are self-paced, while others are more typical with set schedules and deadlines. You may be able to coordinate with your child's school so they receive credit for the course, as opposed to doubling up.

- *Check offerings at your local college.* Sometimes, these institutions offer AP courses to high school students, but your child may need to pay additional fees to enroll. Again, you may be able to work with your child's high school so they can get credit for the class.

- *Help your child go it alone (or almost alone).* Motivated and disciplined students can gather materials and learn on their own before scheduling and taking any AP test. The College Board posts free study guides and past exam questions to help, but this can still be a heavy lift even for the best students. You don't want what happened to Krista, who got a two on her AP Art History exam, to happen to your child. If this is the best option available, consider hiring a tutor for support, enrolling your child in a study group, or both.

Getting Started

Your child can start AP classes as soon as 9th grade, provided they are academically ready to work at a college level and attending a school that offers AP classes to freshmen (many do not). Some AP classes have prerequisites and cannot be taken in freshman year. Individual schools also have their own rules about which classes can be taken when. Many schools may offer AP courses starting in 10th grade, while others may not offer them until 11th grade. If your child's school offers it and they are up to the challenge (or want to attempt to do it outside of school), The College Board recommends AP Human

Geography as a good option for a 9th grader as an introduction to the wider AP program.

How Many APs Are Enough?

There is no magic number of AP classes your child should take to get into a top college. It depends on various factors, including their academic readiness, personal goals, workload capacity, other commitments, and is at least somewhat dependent on what their high school offers. At Ma Academy, we tell most students who hope to attend a top US college to take as many AP classes as they can handle without letting their grades suffer. Usually, by graduation, this means nine or more. Students whose main area of strength is not academic, like athletes, artists, or performers, can get away with as few as three AP classes, preferably that relate to their passions in some way.

Before your child signs up for an AP class, you want to make sure they are academically ready for that class. That means that they should complete prerequisite classes and do well enough in those classes so that they (and you) are confident they're ready to move to the next level. Remember, AP classes are *college-level* classes, meaning they come with an increased rigor that your high school student, especially if they're early on in high school, may not be used to. Taking too many AP classes without the necessary preparation can lead to unnecessary stress and potentially lower grades, which completely defeats the purpose.

When choosing AP classes, your child should first look for courses that align with their passions, supporting their overall academic goals and college aspirations. They (and you) should also consider their strengths and weaknesses in different subjects and think hard about how ready they are to take on the challenge of an AP course in that area. Because of the extra workload involved, your child should aim to spread their AP classes out. If they can start with one AP class freshman year, they can tackle two or three during sophomore year, and split the remaining five or six classes between their last two years of high school. I recommend starting slowly, so your child can get used to the workload and depth of one college-level class, before taking on multiple AP courses simultaneously.

Again, your child's high school will likely have specific policies and guidelines as far as how many AP classes students are allowed to take. Some schools may restrict the number of AP classes your child can take each year (although you can always appeal these rules) or may provide recommendations based on their curriculum and resources. Consult your child's counselor and teachers for guidance on what they recommend based on your child's academic strengths, workload capacity, and personal goals. It can be especially helpful to meet with the teacher who teaches the class as they can outline the expectations of the course so you and your child can determine whether the course is a good fit.

AP classes are one reason top high school students often wind up with a GPA above a "perfect" 4.0. While it depends on the school, they are often graded using a "weighted" scale that awards extra credit due to the difficulty level of the course when compared to a normal high school course. The basic assessments happen the same way, your child's teachers will assess their performance on tests, quizzes, projects, homework assignments, and class participation. The difference is that the final scores are based on a 5.0 scale (or something else) instead of the usual 4.0 scale. In this case, if your child gets an "A" in an AP class, they may receive a weighted grade of 5.0 instead of 4.0.

Getting college credit from the course is a separate issue and related to the standardized AP exam issued by the College Board. Generally, the student must score at least a three out of five, but top schools will require a four or even five to award credit.

The AP Capstone Diploma Program

In 2014, the College Board introduced a special Advanced Placement program designed to provide high school students with a more holistic approach to learning and research to better prepare students for college-level coursework and beyond. The AP Capstone Diploma program is comprised of six courses, including the mandatory AP Seminar and AP Research courses along with four additional courses of the student's choice.

AP Seminar is a year-long course focused on developing critical thinking, research, and presentation skills. Students explore real-world issues from multiple perspectives, write papers, give presentations, and participate in group projects on various topics.

AP Research is another year-long course in which students design, plan, and conduct their own research projects on whatever topic they choose. This is an excellent opportunity for your student to take a deep dive into one of their passions by conducting research on their topic, analyzing collected data, and presenting their findings in both written and oral formats.

If your child decides to pursue the AP Capstone Diploma, their remaining four courses also provide an opportunity to go deep into their passions. If your child chooses wisely, their course selection will tell a clear story of how they pursued their passion and their overall education with commitment and rigor, exactly what college admissions officers want to see.

Of course, there is more than one way to demonstrate rigor through course selection which brings us to...

INTERNATIONAL BACCALAUREATE

The International Baccalaureate (IB) program provides a holistic and rigorous high school curriculum. IB is known for its challenging curriculum focused on developing well-rounded students through an emphasis on critical thinking and global awareness. IB is a demanding (and prestigious) educational option for college-bound students who are seeking a comprehensive and internationally recognized education. IB is currently offered in over 150 countries around the world.

The IB program is offered to students in the final two years of their high school education, although the "Middle Year Program" is sometimes available for students in 9th and 10th grade in preparation for the actual program. It is structured around a comprehensive curriculum that includes languages, sciences, mathematics, humanities, arts, and more. Students take six subjects, including three at a higher level (HL) and three at a standard level (SL), and complete assessments in each subject. While it is a more structured program than AP, there are plenty of options within the IB program to allow your child to focus on their passions and develop skills in those areas.

In addition to the subject-specific curriculum, the IB program also includes three core components:

Theory of Knowledge (TOK): This course focuses on developing critical thinking and inquiry skills and encourages students to reflect on the nature of knowledge, the ways in which knowledge is acquired, and the role of perspective in shaping knowledge.

Extended Essay (EE): This is a research-based essay of up to 4,000 words that allows students to independently explore a topic of their choice within one of the IB subject areas. The Extended Essay requires students to engage with in-depth research, analysis, and synthesis of information. It also provides a perfect opportunity for your student to devote considerable time to their passion. The resulting essay could be submitted with your child's college application packet.

Creativity, Activity, and Service (CAS): Because the International Baccalaureate program is a complete curriculum, it extends into extracurricular activities as well. Students are required to engage in creative, active, and service-oriented pursuits outside of the classroom. The intention is that these diverse activities will promote personal growth, well-being, and social responsibility.

IB classes are graded both by your child's teachers and the IB organization. Teachers grade coursework, essays, oral presentations, and other assignments depending on the subjects being studied. The IB organization also has a series of external assessments including written examinations, practical examinations, and the Extended Essay. The results are used to determine students' final grades in each subject, and the grades are awarded by the IB organization. Students who successfully complete the IB program earn an International Baccalaureate Diploma, which is recognized by colleges and universities around the world, including top US colleges, as a high level of academic achievement that proves they are ready for the challenges of higher education. Additionally, students can earn individual subject certificates for each subject completed.

While the IB program was not designed to replicate specific college courses like AP classes, some top US colleges and universities may grant credit or advanced standing to students who have earned high scores on certain IB assessments. Check with the registrar's offices at your child's target schools to see if they award college credit for any IB classes.

Finally, some students choose to combine AP classes with the IB curriculum. This will depend on your child's high school and on how much work your child can handle, but since IB doesn't start until junior year, your child may be ready to complete a few AP courses throughout their freshman and sophomore years. In the end, the right balance between AP, IB, honors, and regular classes is different for every child. Keep the lines of communication open with your child's counselor, teachers, and your student to find the right balance. As a team, you can find the ideal combination of courses for your child.

Next Steps

If you haven't already, set up an appointment with your child's counselor to discuss their future plans and the best course selection to get them there. Familiarize yourself with the options your child's high school offers. What AP courses are available and when? Is there an IB program? Explore the possibilities with your child and their counselor to determine the right path for them and their goals.

Next, we'll take a closer look at how your child can get the most out of their recommendation letters.

CHAPTER 7

AB WORKOUT #5:

LETTERS OF RECOMMENDATION

William and Kate were high school seniors who had a lot in common. They had similar GPAs and test scores. They were both strong STEM students with a passion for science. Their college applications were thoughtful, each with a clear theme. William showed colleges how he followed his goal of finding a solution to global hunger and the steps he had taken to make it come to fruition. Kate's application, on the other hand, focused on her dream of making clean water accessible to all. Both students played sports at the varsity level and excelled in major science competitions. To top it off, they both had the very same dream school: California Institute of Technology, better known as Caltech.

Sadly, William and Kate never got the opportunity to wait in line together at Browne Dining Hall or compare cheddars at a Cheese Club meeting (yes, Caltech actually has an entire club devoted to cheese). Kate was one of the 3.9 percent of applicants admitted to her dream school, William was not. The difference, believe it or not, may have had very little to do with their actual qualifications.

It may have come down to their letters of recommendation.

At top US schools, every single element of your child's application counts because every applicant has nearly equal qualifications, strong passions, and meaningful achievements. This includes letters of recommendation. All other things being equal, the right recommendation letter can make the difference between admission and rejection. What exactly does the "right" recommendation letter look like, and, more importantly, how do you make sure your child's letters fall into that category? To give you a better idea of what I mean, let's start by comparing William's and Kate's letters of recommendation.

This was William's recommendation letter.

To Whom It May Concern,

I am writing to recommend William for admission to Caltech. He has been a diligent and committed student during his time at West High School.

I have known William for several years as he has pursued advanced studies in chemistry and biology. He has consistently performed well in his classes, maintaining a solid GPA, making the Honor Roll every year, and demonstrating a broad understanding of the subject matter. He has shown consistent effort in attending class, completing assignments on time, and actively participating in class discussions. He has also sought help and clarification when needed, displaying a proactive approach to learning.

In addition to William's academic performance, he has been involved in a number of extracurricular activities and has shown leadership potential. He earned high honors in the Science Olympiad and is an all-star forward on our school's varsity soccer team. He also served as Treasurer of our student body, demonstrating good organizational skills, leadership, and dedication.

Furthermore, William has shown admirable interpersonal skills, getting along well with both peers and faculty. He is respectful, polite, and professional in his interactions and has shown a willingness to collaborate and support others.

Overall, I believe that William Lee would be a valuable addition to the Caltech student body. He has demonstrated consistent academic performance, leadership potential, and positive inter-personal skills. I am pleased to recommend him for admission, and I am confident that he will excel in his academic pursuits.

Should you require any additional information, please do not hesitate to contact me.

Sincerely,

William's Teacher

After reading that, you might be wondering what could possibly be wrong with it. It says some very nice, complimentary things about William. It certainly doesn't raise any red flags or say anything negative.

Let's contrast William's recommendation letter with Kate's rec-ommendation letter:

To Whom It May Concern,

I am writing to highly recommend Kate for admission to Caltech. As Kate's teacher and mentor for the past three years at East High School, I have been thoroughly impressed with her exceptional academic achievements, leadership skills, and unwavering dedication to making a positive impact in the field of science.

Kate has demonstrated remarkable excellence in both academics and extracurricular activities. As the captain of our varsity women's basketball team, she has exhibited exceptional leadership qualities, inspiring her team members to excel both on and off the court. She has also shown exemplary dedication to her studies, maintaining top grades in all her science and mathematics courses, and consistently earning a place on the honor roll.

One of Kate's most notable achievements is her exceptional performance in national science competitions. She has won multiple awards in the highly competitive Google Science Fair and National Science Bowl, showcasing her ingenuity, creativity, and scientific acumen. Her project titled "Developing a Novel Eco-Friendly Approach for Sustainable Water Purification Using Nanotechnology" is a testament to her innovative thinking and dedication to addressing real-world issues. Kate's research involved synthesizing biodegradable nanoparticles from renewable sources and evaluating their effectiveness in removing water contaminants, including heavy metals and organic pollutants. Her results were outstanding, demonstrating a high level of scientific rigor and practical applications, with potential for scalable implementation in real-world scenarios.

What truly sets Kate apart is her unwavering passion for giving people access to clean water. Her project was motivated by a deep-seated desire to address the global issue of water scarcity and pollution, and her innovative approach using nanotechnology reflects her commitment to finding sustainable and eco-friendly solutions. Kate has also been actively involved in community service initiatives related to water conservation and awareness, volunteering her time and expertise to educate and engage others in understanding the importance of clean water and its impact on society.

Apart from her impressive achievements, Kate is an exceptional individual with outstanding personal qualities. She is a self-motivated, curious, and dedicated learner, always seeking ways to expand her knowledge and skills. She is also an excellent communicator, both in writing and verbally, and has the ability to articulate complex scientific concepts in a clear and concise manner. Her positive attitude, perseverance, and teamwork skills make her a valuable asset to any academic or extracurricular team.

In conclusion, I have no doubt that Kate will excel in her academic pursuits and continue to make meaningful contributions to the field of science. Her exceptional achievements, passion for clean water access, and outstanding personal qualities make her a standout candidate for admission to Caltech. I highly recommend Kate without any reservations and believe she will be a valuable addition to your academic community.

Please feel free to contact me for any further information or references. Thank you for considering Kate's application.

Sincerely,

Kate's Teacher

Notice the difference? William's letter, while complimentary, basically reads like a recitation of a list of facts that are *already right there on his application.* There's no real insight into what makes him tick or what he's like as a person. Kate's letter, on the other hand, paints a more complete picture of Kate's work, her passion for that work, the results she's garnered, and her goals to continue this work in the future.

Everything else being equal, which student would you admit?

That's why the fifth element of your child's six-pack, and the focus of this chapter, is getting the most out of their letters of recommendation.

What Is a Letter of Recommendation?

At its core, a letter of recommendation for college admission is basically a written endorsement of a student's character, abilities, and potential from the perspective of an adult authority figure, usually a teacher. School counselors, coaches or other trusted adults who have had a significant impact on the student's academic or personal growth may also write a letter of recommendation. The letter should highlight the student's strengths, achievements, and unique qualities, providing insights beyond what can be gleaned from transcripts and test scores. This insight from a respected figure who knows your child well is exactly what admissions officers are looking for during the seven to fifteen minutes they spend "with" your child as they review their application.

These letters are like a third-party evaluation of your student's qualities and potential for success in college, giving an admissions officer "professional" insights into their character, abilities, and potential. It can reinforce your child's application theme and help them rise above the competition. A strong letter of recommendation, like Kate's, works the way a good application essay (which we'll get to in the very next chapter) does. It goes beyond detailing your child's accomplishments and activities to say something about who your child is as a human being, what they are passionate about, what makes them special, and most importantly, why they are a good candidate for admission to whatever college or university they are applying to. Coming from a trustworthy adult, these letters become a powerful tool.

A recommendation letter serves the following purposes in the college admissions process:

- *Provides additional perspective:* A well-written letter of recommendation from a teacher, counselor, or other trusted individual can provide insights and perspectives about the applicant that may not be apparent from their academic records or application materials. It can shed light on the applicant's personal qualities, meaning their personality, work ethic, leadership skills, and values relevant to their potential success in college.

- *Validates qualifications:* Recommendation letters from respected professionals confirm a student's potential to succeed in college. They serve as evidence of their academic abilities, motivation, and achievements, and can provide assurance to the admissions committee that the applicant is a good fit for the college or program they are applying to.

- *Differentiates the applicant:* Think about how Kate's letter of recommendation made her look like a stronger candidate than William, even though they were equally qualified. By focusing on specifics like her accomplishments, experiences, and goals, Kate's letter painted a clearer (and better) picture of who she was as a person.

- *Reinforces the application theme:* The best recommendation letters read like chapters in the applicant's larger story. By sharing a different perspective on their skills, passions, and dreams, while highlighting their unique experiences, letters of recommendation show how your child will be a valuable addition to the college community.

- *Provides evidence of character:* A letter from a qualified adult who knows your child well can provide evidence of your child's integrity and personal qualities that are important for college success, such as leadership, resilience, initiative, and maturity.

- *Offers insight regarding academic strength:* Like William and Kate, your child will probably compete with a group of students with similar grades and test scores. Additional insight into who your child is in the classroom often makes a difference because it shows your student is the type of student future professors will be excited to teach!

- *Builds credibility:* A well-written letter of recommendation from a respected and credible source, like a teacher or counselor, is basically an external endorsement of your child's qualifications. It tells the admissions officer, *"it's okay to trust what you're reading in this application. This kid is legit."*

Cultivating Recommender Relationships

For your child to have the kind of relationships with adults that lead to effective recommendation letters, they need to feel somewhat comfortable in the adult world. They need to be able to talk to their teachers, supervisors, coaches, and other authority figures in their lives to build positive relationships. This process should start at the beginning of high school, not when the college application becomes available. While this isn't always easy, every child should try to:

- Be engaged and participate actively in class or other activities. Tell your child to show genuine interest in the subject matter, ask questions, and contribute to class discussions. This shows teachers that your child is actively engaged in their own learning process.

- Show respect and professionalism. It should go without saying that your child should treat everyone, especially adults, with respect. Remind them to be courteous, polite, and professional in their interactions. Disruptive or disrespectful behavior in school will negatively impact an applicant's candidacy.

- Seek help and ask for feedback. Adults are great resources with broad wisdom; encourage your child to seek guidance, show initiative, and take responsibility for their own learning and success. Adults want to help students who are willing to listen, learn, and grow. They will be more likely to provide meaningful feedback and support to a child who seems open to it.

- Meet deadlines and follow instructions. This should be a no-brainer. Top colleges expect students to perform well, so your child should already be accustomed to doing careful work and submitting their assignments on time. This shows adults your child is responsible, reliable, and takes their commitments seriously.

- Be proactive and communicate effectively. If your child has concerns or questions, they should speak up respectfully.

- Show appreciation and express gratitude. If your child takes time to express appreciation and gratitude to the adults in their life, either in person or through a handwritten note, those adults are more likely to feel good about your child and form a stronger relationship with them. Those strong relationships can lead to some powerful recommendation letters down the line.

Teach your children these skills early, so they can do this on their own once they reach the end of high school. One way to help is by encouraging them to see the adults in their lives not as scary authority figures, but as caring, interested people who are there to help them prepare for the challenges ahead.

FINDING RECOMMENDERS

Most schools ask for two letters of recommendation, and the most obvious choice to write at least one of them is your child's favorite teacher. In fact, many top US colleges and universities require a letter from a teacher who taught your child in their class, usually in a core academic area like English, math, science, social studies, or a foreign language. Within those parameters, your goal should be to find those teachers who know your child best, have the strongest relationships with your child, and are most closely connected to your child's passion, so they can share aspects of your child's story with authority and provide some "official" reinforcement of their theme.

Colleges want letters from teachers who worked with your child in 10th, 11th, or 12th grade, although I personally think 12th grade is far too late in the process to approach someone new and request a letter. In my opinion, your child should be thinking about their teachers as potential recommenders from the get-go, which means engaging with them while they're in class and staying in contact with former teachers who played an important role in their high school experience throughout high school. Encourage your student to keep these relationships strong so those teachers remain invested in your child's success. The goal for your child is to have a team of teachers behind them, all of whom know exactly why your child is special. This way, you will ensure the teachers who write the letters of recommendation will know your child well enough to paint a convincing picture of why they are a strong candidate for admission to the school of their choice.

When the time comes for your child to ask their teacher(s) for a recommendation, think about the following:

- Who is the most natural fit to promote your child to the college or program they want to attend? For example, if your child is applying to a selective creative writing program, they will likely want a letter from their favorite English teacher. Look for a teacher who has a unique perspective on your child's abilities and interests and can offer insights into your child that aren't mentioned elsewhere in the application.

- Who has played the biggest role in your child's growth, experiences, and accomplishments within the realm of their passion and application theme? Teachers who have been partners with your child on this part of their academic journey are ideal candidates to flesh out your child's story, giving it power and credibility.

- Who is most excited about your child's unique accomplishments, skills, and character and can speak about them in a positive and specific manner? Letters from teachers who know your child well enough to speak in detail about their strengths and potential are more effective than letters from those who can vouch for your child's accomplishments on paper but may not have had a deep level of interaction with your child.

WORKING WITH RECOMMENDERS

To make this process as easy as possible for your child's teachers (or other recommenders), your student should approach them about writing a letter as early as possible. Remember, your child is probably not the only student requesting a recommendation letter from their favorite teacher, so the earlier they can get started, the better. If the teacher is open to it, have your student schedule a quick meeting to talk about the schools they are applying to and the ones they're most hoping to attend, as well as their application theme and the general story they're trying to tell. They should bring their essays to the meeting to help the recommender familiarize themselves with that story, along with their transcript, test scores, resumé, and application deadlines.

In addition to the required teacher letter, students can submit a letter from another adult of their choosing. This additional letter can be from a teacher, supervisor, coach, or mentor who knows them well. Your child should look for a recommender who has seen evidence of how they think, what they're good at, and what they care about. The one exception to this rule is if your child can line up a second recommender with some clout, like the principal, city councilman, or an alumnus of the school they hope to attend. Having that seal of approval can give your child's application an extra boost. If there is a "power recommender" in your child's life, ensure at least one of their other recommenders can describe who your child is and what they're passionate about with some kind of authority.

Counselor Letters

If your child is a student at a private or international high school, the relationship they cultivate with their counselor may be as important as the ones they build with their teachers. Like so many other things in this book, that's something that should start early in (or even before) your child's freshman year. School counselors have a clear picture of who your child is and what matters to them, so a letter from a counselor can be a great "introductory" letter in your student's application.

You will likely meet with your child's counselor regardless of whether you need a letter from them, as part of your child's college planning process. To make sure you get things off on the right foot (and keep them there), make sure you, as a parent, do the following:

- Show up to any parent information sessions the school counselors hold to discuss the college process

- Complete questionnaires and other paperwork requested by the counseling office in a timely manner

- Come to college counseling meetings prepared with the proper documentation and relevant questions

- Remain cooperative and responsive throughout the process

Keep in mind that when applying to college in the US, students waive their right to see their letters of recommendation once they ask a teacher to write the same. That means they won't be able to make corrections or update information, so it's crucial that they give their letter-writers all the relevant information and talking points discussed above. Since not all recommenders are great at meeting deadlines, make sure your child has a backup just in case.

If your child has many potential recommenders, they can approach more people than they will ultimately need to gauge who is most available and interested in writing a letter for them. Your child can talk with their teachers and other potential recommenders about the possibility of writing a letter for them, to get a sense of who has something interesting to say or seems enthusiastic about singing their praises. Some recommenders may be more willing than others, some may have more time, some may have had more significant experiences

TAKE THE TIME TO FIND SOMEONE WHO KNOWS YOUR CHILD WELL AND IS WILLING AND HAPPY TO TELL THEIR STORY.

with your child. It can be a bit of a balancing act, so make sure your child talks with each of their potential recommenders in advance to get a sense of how they feel about the "job." By taking the time and putting in the thought to find recommenders who know them well and are happy to tell their story , your child can ensure their letters of recommendation paint the best, clearest, and most powerful picture of who they are and what they have to offer.

When submitting their letters, make sure your child adheres to the application guidelines provided by each college or program. Some may have specific instructions on the number of letters to submit or the types of recommenders they prefer. It is essential to follow these requirements for your child to receive a strong evaluation by an admissions officer.

Next Steps

Now that you know everything you could ever want to know about recommendation letters, you and your child can get serious about the process of obtaining the right ones. Start thinking about the teachers, coaches, counselors, leaders, and other important adults in their life, especially adults who are connected to your child's passion, and nurture those relationships. Help your child feel comfortable interacting with adults outside of the family and encourage them to ask these other adults for advice, guidance, and help. Be proactive and address any shyness or behavior issues your child exhibits now, so your child can focus on building a deep bench of potential recommenders who know, like, and can vouch for them.

In the next chapter, we'll take a deep dive into the most pivotal aspect of your child's college application: their application essay(s).

CHAPTER 8

AB WORKOUT #6:

COLLEGE ESSAYS

Out of all the elements included in a college application, none is more powerful, impactful, and therefore angst-inducing than the college essay. But don't take my word for it. Take it from *The New York Times*, which called application essays the most important "soft factor" in college admissions (and the fourth most important factor overall, after high school GPA, curriculum strength, and standardized test scores).[22]

College essays are powerful because they let your child introduce themselves to the admissions officer. A well-written essay can reveal your child's character, capabilities, and thought processes in a way no other element of their application can. At the same time, it allows your child to "frame the narrative" by elaborating on their application theme in detail. If there are any weak points in their educational or personal history, a college essay can also be used to address those areas and provide context within the application theme. On the other hand,

---

22 Arvind Ashok, "The persistent grip of social class on college admissions," *The New York Times,* May 26, 2021, https://www.nytimes.com/2021/05/26/upshot/college-admissions-essay-sat.html.

if your child's high school record is one amazing accomplishment after another, their essay is the best opportunity to give these achievements context. Your child should use this space to tell the story of how they developed their passion, discuss an impactful experience they had while pursuing their passion, or elucidate where and how they hope to continue exploring their passion in college.

If the upside of the college essay is space and freedom for your student to tell their story, the downside is that the same. The inherently unstructured nature of the prompt causes a lot of anxiety and stress to write the "perfect" essay. Even students who are strong and confident writers will struggle with the power of the personal statement and pressure to get it "right." Typically, college essays are 250 to 650 words, at least on the Common App, which is not a huge amount of space to get it "right" in. Every sentence counts, so producing the best essay possible takes work: framing the flow of their journey, sharing the right stories, choosing the most compelling details, and making it as interesting as possible to read. Don't forget, this is all while using the perfect syntax, grammar, and a touch of humor and humility! To add insult to injury, the personal statement is often the first time your student has ever been asked to write a thoughtful, detailed essay about themselves. It's a tall order, to say the least. This chapter is designed to help your child (and you) tackle this challenge with confidence.

Essay Writing 101

Before we go any further, if your child struggles at all with writing (and even if they don't), I highly recommend getting them some extra help in this area. This does not mean I suggest you hire someone to write their essays for them or have them feed their prompt and some personal details into an AI chatbot and submit whatever it spits out. While these options might look tempting, admissions officers aren't stupid. Most of them can spot work that has been "professionally penned" or computer-generated. College essay prompts don't vary much, and some of these "for-hire" essays are often re-sold and re-used over and over again. Even if you have the money to pony up for a genuine, crafted-from-scratch original essay for your child, remember that if they are admitted, their real writing abilities will be on display for everyone at that college to see. If they can't keep up with the expected writing level at their college or university, they are going to struggle. Both ethically and academically, using these options could lead to problems down the line. Instead, do whatever you can to boost your child's writing skills rather than rely on someone else's. Of course, you can hire an essay coach to work with your child; just keep in mind that the coach should be helping your child create their best work, *not* doing it for them.

When it comes to what to include in a college application essay, it's easier to define the opposite: what not to write about. Your child should not spend 650 words reiterating the same information about their perfect GPA or impressive record of activities that the admissions officer will see in other parts of their application. "Real estate" is limited in the college application, so use the essay to dig deeper and expand beyond what is listed elsewhere. The point of the college essay is to make the facts and figures part of the larger story of who your child is and why they deserve admission to the school of their dreams. Essays are opportunities for your child to demonstrate why they want to go to that school, what they value in life, how they solve problems, how they see the world, and above all, what makes them unique. How can they do this all in less than 650 words? By telling thoughtful stories showcasing their passions.

That's the *other* upside of all the hard work of writing a college essay: it's the only aspect of your child's college application they can completely control. They are free to use it however they like; to spotlight an achievement, demonstrate a talent, explain a passion, or even tackle a combo of these. More importantly, as I mentioned earlier, if your child needs it, their essay can also be used for damage control, a way to "spin" past problems into resilience and growth.

Even if your child isn't the greatest or most confident writer, they can make their essay about it: how they've dealt with the problem, how they've achieved despite their weakness, and how this resilience will translate to success as a college student. Herein lies the power of the college essay. Your child can tell an admissions officer directly why they should be admitted, painting the exact picture they want to paint. Just because your child doesn't have shelves full of awards or a perfect GPA doesn't mean they don't have a compelling story to tell. The college essay is their place to shine.

ESSAY TOPICS

The Common App requires applicants to write a *personal statement*. The personal statement is a general essay allowing applicants to share their personal story, experiences, and perspectives with college admissions officers. In other words, it's an ideal set-up for your child to introduce and explain their application theme.

In addition to the personal statement, the Common App also includes several other prompts that some schools may require applicants to answer. These prompts are known as "supplemental essays." Supplemental essays may ask about a particular theme or require applicants to respond to specific questions about the college or program they are applying to. It's important to note that application requirements may vary by college. Always confirm the specific requirements of each college you're applying to through the Common App's or college's website to ensure you are following their guidelines and submitting all required information, including essays and documents.

These are the Common App essay prompts for the 2023–2024 application year (They rarely change in any significant way.):

1. Some students have a background, identity, interest, or talent that is so meaningful they believe their application would be incomplete without it. If this sounds like you, then please share your story.

2. The lessons we take from obstacles we encounter can be fundamental to later success. Recount a time when you faced a challenge, setback, or failure. How did it affect you, and what did you learn from the experience?

3. Reflect on a time when you questioned or challenged a belief or idea. What prompted your thinking? What was the outcome?

4. Reflect on something that someone has done for you that has made you happy or thankful in a surprising way. How has this gratitude affected or motivated you?

5. Discuss an accomplishment, event, or realization that sparked a period of personal growth and a new understanding of yourself or others.

6. Describe a topic, idea, or concept you find so engaging that it makes you lose all track of time. Why does it captivate you? What or who do you turn to when you want to learn more?

7. Share an essay on any topic of your choice. It can be one you've already written, one that responds to a different prompt, or one of your own design.

Notice that the first six prompts provided on the Common App are all open-ended, giving students a starting point to tell a story or share an experience or opinion that is meaningful to them. College essays aren't like those your child writes in English Lit or American History class with claims and evidence to back them up. Instead, they're about the unique way your child interprets the question and relates it to their own life, revealing aspects of their personality, their interests, and the way their mind works in the process.

Of note, I am wary the final prompt where students can submit an already-written essay or personalized prompt. My advice is to utilize this option with caution. Unless your child has already written an essay that reflects their application theme and showcases who they are in the most compelling way possible, they're likely better off crafting a new essay with their passion and application theme in mind. If your child has an amazing, award-winning essay they're especially proud of, make sure they update it, show it to their advisors for feedback, and make any necessary final improvements before it is submitted, just like they would with a brand-new college essay.

HOW TO WRITE A COLLEGE ESSAY

There's an old saying that all writing is rewriting. Writing a good college essay is no exception. Your child should expect to go through several stages of writing and rewriting before their essay is considered "finished," following these basic steps:

1. Brainstorming: Your child should begin by simply brainstorming a bunch of ideas for their essay. Talk with them about which prompts provide the best opportunity for them to illustrate their application theme, as well as the experiences, accomplishments, passions, and goals that support

their story. Help your child zero in on what makes them unique and what they want to convey to the admissions committee. Encourage them to jot down ideas and explore different perspectives.

2. Outlining: Once your child has chosen a prompt and has a clear idea of their essay's focus, the next step is to create an outline. Outlining helps writers stay organized and ensures the essay has a coherent structure. The best essays are well-organized. They begin with an introduction that sets up the points your child will be making in the essay, which is followed by body paragraphs where they will make those points, and finally conclude the essay by tying everything together.

3. Writing: Once your child has a strong outline, they are ready for a first draft. Make it clear to your child that this stage is not about perfection, it's just about getting words on paper as a starting point. In this draft, your child should write freely and let their ideas flow without worrying about being "good enough." All they need to do at this stage is follow their outline and expand on those ideas with specific details and examples. If they follow this process, they should wind up with a solid first draft.

4. Revising: Once your child finishes their first draft, it's time for them to take a break and do something else. This way, when they come back to their essay in a day or so, it will be with "fresh eyes." It's easier to review their essay more critically and make revisions for clarity, coherence, and effectiveness when revising a few days after writing. At this point, they must check for spelling and grammatical errors. Finally,

I encourage them to read the essay out loud, because this will help them identify areas that don't flow smoothly. They can even read it aloud to you or other adults they trust to garner constructive feedback.

5. Editing: Once your child is happy about what their essay says, the next step is to make it pretty. Besides editing for spelling and grammar, they should refine their sentences, trimming unnecessary words to ensure their essay is delivered concisely and impactfully.

6. Polishing: After editing, your child should re-read their essay to make sure it reflects their application theme and makes the points they hope to make in. At this point, they can make any final tweaks to the style, tone, and overall flow. Remind your child to include a strong introduction hooking the reader and introducing their application theme, a compelling body that supports their main points, and a conclusion that leaves a lasting impression while simultaneously tying the essay together. Finally, ensure the editing process doesn't remove their natural voice from the essay because that voice and personality are, ultimately, what the essay is supposed to showcase.

7. Proofreading: Once the essay has been polished, your child should thoroughly proofread it one last time looking for typos, misspellings, and formatting issues. Remind them to read the essay carefully and slowly to catch any remaining mistakes. As a parent, you may also want to give the essay a second proofread, just to be safe, before other people get a chance to read it.

8. Seeking Feedback: After proofreading, the next step is for your child to share their essay with some trusted advisors (other than you) and ask for constructive feedback. Look for trusted sources like their teachers, counselors, and other mentors who know your child well. Once they provide their insights and suggestions for improvement, your child should revise the essay appropriately to strengthen their essay.

9. Final Review: Once your child has completed the last round of revisions and edits, they should do a final review of their essay. Have them read it aloud to catch any last-minute errors or awkward phrasing and do the same yourself. Ensure that the essay falls within the word limit, follows the prompt, and aligns with the values and mission of the college or university your child is applying to.

By the time your child finishes these steps, their essay should clearly reflect exactly what they want to say about themselves and what matters to them. As a parent, remind your child to start early, be mindful of deadlines as the revising process can be lengthy, and provide them with reassurance that the final result will be worth the effort.

Essays: the Good, the Bad, and the Ugly

What does it look like when the end results are actually worth all that effort? And what does it look like when an essay falls short? Compare these two personal statements from two similarly qualified students, both of whom hope to pursue careers in social justice. Let's begin with the weaker essay.

Social justice has always been a driving force in my life. From a young age, I've been passionate about advocating for those who are marginalized or facing inequality. I believe that everyone deserves equal opportunities and fair treatment, and I am committed to making a positive impact in the world.

In high school, I engaged in a variety of activities related to social justice. I volunteered at a local food bank regularly and participated in several awareness campaigns on social media to raise awareness about issues such as racial justice, LGBTQ+ rights, and gender equality. I also attended local events and workshops on social justice topics to further educate myself and deepen my understanding of the challenges faced by marginalized communities.

One of the highlights of my social justice involvement was spearheading a fundraising campaign for a local homeless shelter during my junior year. I organized a charity event at my school, leveraging social media and other channels to raise awareness and garner support. Despite facing challenges and setbacks, including difficulties in securing funding and navigating logistics, I remained committed to the cause and worked tirelessly to make the campaign a success. In the end, we were able to exceed our fundraising goal and make a meaningful impact on the homeless community in our area.

In addition to my extracurricular involvement, I have maintained a high GPA throughout high school and scored well on standardized tests. However, my academic achievements have not detracted from my passion for social justice. In fact, I believe that my academic excellence provides me with a solid founda-

tion to further pursue my career in social justice and make a meaningful impact in the field.

Looking ahead, I am eager to continue my pursuit of social justice in college and beyond. I plan to explore opportunities to get involved in social justice-related activities on campus, such as joining clubs, participating in volunteer programs, and engaging with advocacy groups. I am also excited about the prospect of taking relevant courses to deepen my knowledge and understanding of social justice issues and gain the skills needed to effect positive change.

I am aware that pursuing a career in social justice may come with challenges and complexities. However, I am committed to overcoming these obstacles and making a lasting impact in the field. I am determined to use my skills, knowledge, and passion to advocate for positive change and contribute to creating a more just and equitable society.

In conclusion, social justice is a fundamental aspect of my identity and my life's purpose. I have been actively involved in social justice-related activities in high school, including spearheading a successful fundraising campaign for a local homeless shelter. While my academic achievements have been strong, they have not deterred me from my commitment to social justice. I am excited about the opportunities that lie ahead in college and beyond, and I am determined to continue my pursuit of a career in social justice and make a meaningful impact in the world.

When you read that essay, you might not be able to pinpoint anything specific that "feels" wrong. It talks about the student's passion for social justice, their strong grades, and even details many of the activities they participated in over the course of their high school years. So why, exactly, is this a weak personal statement? Let's get into a few reasons:

1. It's not specific. The essay mentions involvement in multiple social justice activities, including volunteering at a food bank, participating in awareness campaigns, and organizing a fundraising campaign for a homeless shelter. However, it lacks specific details or anecdotes that bring those experiences to life and illustrate their impact on the student. Admissions officers like to use the following analogy: if your child's life is a field, they should choose one or two individual blades of grass from that entire field to focus on in the essay. The personal statement is short, so drill into the minutiae to leave a lasting impact on the reader.

2. It's not reflective. The essay does not delve deeply into the student's personal reflections or insights regarding their experiences in social justice activities. The lack of introspection leaves the admissions officer wondering what this student really gained from these experiences.

3. It's not future-focused. While the essay briefly mentions the student's plan to pursue social justice activities in college and beyond, it does not clearly articulate how their past experiences and achievements have prepared them for their future career in social justice, or what they hope to do next.

4. It lacks personality. The essay uses general language and cliches, like "making a meaningful impact in the world," without providing specific examples or unique perspectives to differentiate this student from another student with similar interests.

In a nutshell, this is why the above essay is unlikely to help that student gain admission to a top school. Now let's consider this stronger personal statement:

Everybody goes to college for their own reason: to get a degree, to get a great job, because it's a rite of passage to adulthood. I want to go to college—to Brown, specifically—because I want to change the world. Or, at least, I want to be a part of changing the world for unhoused people everywhere. And Brown seems like the ideal place for me to start making that dream come true.

I have been working with unhoused people ever since I was a kid, when my parents brought me to the local soup kitchen at Thanksgiving and Christmas. While they served up plates of turkey and dressing, I talked to the people they were serving. I was so curious about their lives. Where did they come from? How did they end up in such desperate circumstances? The more I learned, the more I wanted to help, and by the time I got to high school, I had already volunteered with several local organizations that provided shelter and support services to unhoused people.

Then I found Helping House, one of the only pet-friendly shelters in my city, and I wound up staying for two years—right through today. My duties there include everything from assisting with meal preparations to cleaning to organizing donations, but for me, the best part has been getting to know the residents. I love talking with Mary, who used to be an actress, about her time in the movies and her grandchildren who live across the country. I look forward to the days when I get to accompany George, who served in the Gulf War, on walks with his dog, Mr. Bones. Getting to know these people as actual human beings with hearts and souls and dreams has helped me gain clarity about where society is failing them, and what they need and want from their community that they aren't getting.

My work at Helping House inspired me to launch a campaign at my high school that collected essential items, such as blankets and toiletries, that the residents told me they needed but rarely received. The day I brought those cases of shampoo and nail clippers to my friends at the shelter was one of the happiest days of my life. It also gave me clarity about what I want to do with the rest of my life—to dedicate myself to helping people like Mary and George get out of shelters and into safe, permanent homes. I want to study the root causes of homelessness, like systemic inequalities and lack of affordable housing, so that I can help create better solutions for people who are struggling.

That's why I'm so excited about the possibility of attending college at Brown. When I read about the Hope at Brown program, I ran and showed my mother! The opportunity to continue my advocacy work on behalf of the unhoused by doing on-the-ground research with a whole team of students just like me almost sounds like a dream. If accepted, I also plan to major in Political Science with a concentration in Public Policy, hopefully securing an internship in local government or homeless advocacy, so I can prepare for a career in the field.

I've spent the last four years of my life trying to change the world, and I know in my heart that Brown is the best possible place for me to take my quest to the next level and maybe, actually, make a real difference in people's lives.

Wow, admit that student! Let me explain what this student did in the essay that also made you want to accept this student to your university:

1. It shows passion and dedication. The essay clearly demonstrates the student's genuine and unwavering passion for a specific cause: helping the homeless. It conveys their deep commitment to social justice through their involvement in various organizations and plans for future engagement. The use of confident and assertive language conveys the student's conviction and determination to make a meaningful difference.

2. It demonstrates deep personal reflection. The student demonstrates their passion for helping the homeless and the impact this engagement has had in their own life. It shows their understanding that solving homelessness is a complex and evolving challenge that will require continuous learning and creative solutions.

3. It emphasizes clear goals and aspirations. The essay outlines the student's specific goals and aspirations for college, including their reasons for wanting to attend that specific school! This is great for an Early Decision or Early Action essay. By noting specific programs unique to Brown, the student also shows why Brown is right for them and demonstrates how they will elevate these communities as a future student.

4. It highlights learning and collaboration. This student is eager to engage with diverse perspectives, learn from accomplished faculty, and collaborate with like-minded peers. The student recognizes that ending homelessness will require collaborative efforts.

5. The writing is coherent and concise. The essay is well-structured and effectively conveys the student's message in a concise manner within the word limit. Without distracting errors, the focus is on the student's engagement and passion. The use of specific examples and confident language adds credibility and impact to the essay.

Overall, the essay is strong because it shows who this student is, what they care about, and what they hope to contribute to their college community. It showcases the student's commitment, maturity, and readiness to help make positive change. These qualities are very appealing to admissions committees evaluating applicants.

Tips for Writing a Strong Essay

Hopefully, this chapter hasn't made the essay-writing process even scarier for your child. The reality is, if they allow themselves enough time and get the proper support, any child who is talented enough to consider a top-tier US college should be able to write a convincing essay that makes the case for why they deserve admission. As a final word on the subject, advise your child to follow these tips:

1. Be Authentic: Avoid writing what they think the admissions committees want to hear, focusing instead on their own voice and experiences. Authenticity can make your child's essay stand out, after all, there's only one of them in the world!

2. Follow the Prompt: Make sure your child carefully reads and understands the essay prompt provided by the college or university and ensures their essay addresses the prompt directly and effectively. Tailor the essay to carefully fit the

selected prompt. This demonstrates your child's ability to follow instructions and meet the requirements.

3. Show, Don't Tell: Encourage your child to use specific examples and vivid details to illustrate their experiences, accomplishments, and insights. Instead of stating facts, aim to show exactly how these experiences shaped them and what they learned. Consider how the second essay discussed specific people at the homeless shelter. These kinds of details will make your child's essay more engaging and memorable.

4. Be Concise and Coherent: Every word counts. There is not enough space for repetitive phrases, vague statements, and irrelevant information. Stay focused and well-organized with a clear introduction, body, and conclusion.

5. Reflect and Self-Reflect: Your child should share their reflections on the experience they write about to demonstrate self-awareness. Encourage them to reflect on their values, beliefs, and motivations related to the topic of their essay. This can help the admissions committee understand your child's character and potential for growth.

6. Be Positive and Optimistic: Remind your child to emphasize their strengths, achievements, and aspirations. While they can certainly use an essay to address and explain potential weaknesses, they should navigate this carefully, avoiding negative statements or complaints. Instead, ensure your child focuses on the personal qualities like enthusiasm, motivation, and resilience that they developed because of this hurdle.

7. Seek Feedback: As I mentioned earlier, your child should seek out feedback from trusted teachers, counselors, and/or other

mentors for their honest opinions. Outsiders can provide your child with valuable insights they may have missed, as well as suggestions for improvement. However, your child should also be careful about having too many cooks in the kitchen. You don't want your child to lose their unique voice by allowing too many outsiders to chime in with theirs, so look for consensus in the suggestions and remind them not to feel compelled to address every single piece of advice.

8. Be Mindful of Tone and Language: This can be tricky. Your child should choose the appropriate tone and language for their essay, while at the same time, being themselves. They should be professional, avoiding both slang and formal academic language. Stick to a polite tone with syntax comprised of your student's daily vernacular.

9. Be Aware of Your Audience: You child should keep in mind that their essay will be read by college admissions officers with the sole purpose of evaluating their application. If possible, your child should tailor their essays (especially the school-specific supplemental essays) to the specific colleges and universities they are applying to. This means researching the school's values, mission, and programs in advance to incorporate into their essays.

10. Start Early and Revise Often: I've said it before, but I can't stress it enough. Your child MUST give themselves ample time to brainstorm, write, revise, and polish their essay. Multiple times. The earlier your child gets started, the more time they will have to reflect on their experiences and add to the final product, gather feedback, and make multiple revisions to ensure their essay is strong and compelling.

Remember, your child's college essays represent the ultimate opportunity for them to showcase their unique qualities, experiences, passions, and aspirations. While strong writing matters, ensuring your child is true to themselves, demonstrates their passion, reflects on their experiences, and communicates effectively will ultimately matter more than being the world's best writer. These factors will help

> **WHILE STRONG WRITING OF COURSE MATTERS, WHAT MATTERS EVEN MORE IS THAT YOUR CHILD IS TRUE TO THEMSELVES.**

convince their admissions officers that your child should be admitted into the incoming class.

Next Steps

Help your child begin the brainstorming process by talking with them about the story they want to tell in their personal statement. Look at the Common App's most recent essay prompts and talk with your child about which ones speak to their experiences, goals, and passions. If your child struggles with writing, now is the time to hire a coach or tutor to help them get more comfortable with the process. It won't just matter on their applications, but also in the future, when they are writing college essays *in* college.

This was the final component of your child's six-pack, so now it's time to move on to the admission process. In the next chapter, we'll look at what happens to your child's college application once it's submitted.

CHAPTER 9

HOW THE ADMISSIONS PROCESS WORKS

While you and your child likely understand the general steps to apply to college, the process following submission is murkier. To make this clearer, let's explore the "journey" of your child's application and the steps the admissions office will take to decide whether to admit your child to their school. Keep in mind that this is a general overview, as individual schools often vary.

Step 1: Initial Review

When a student submits their application, it will typically trigger an *applicant portal* to be set up. Most, but not all, top US colleges use a system where your student will have their own portal where they will be able to see that all their materials have been received, and if anything is missing, like test scores, a recommendation, or a transcript.

The school will likely reach out when they notice missing materials or if there are any other issues, however, encourage your child to be proactive by checking the status of their application and reaching out to the admissions office themselves if they have any questions or concerns. It's always a good idea to check with the admissions office of each school your child is interested in beforehand to learn how they handle communication with applicants during the initial review process. This information is typically found on the admissions office website or the FAQ section.

Step 2: Primary Review

Once your child's application is deemed "complete," it is evaluated by an admissions officer who looks over all the basics we've discussed in this book: GPA, test scores, extracurricular activities, personal statement, supplemental essays, recommendation letters, and other supporting documents. At top schools, this evaluation is very comprehensive. The admissions officer will use this material to look for evidence of your child's passion, assess their personal qualities like leadership, creativity, problem solving, and community involvement, and finally make their seven-minute decision as to whether the applicant is a good fit for the school. If your child's application fails to pass this initial test, its journey ends here.

Step 3: Second Review

If your child's application makes it through the primary review phase, the next step is for a formal admissions committee or additional reviewers to take a deeper dive and give the application an additional evaluation. Other admissions officials, faculty members, administrators, and sometimes even current students may be involved in this phase of the review process. The goal is to determine which students are the best fit to contribute to the campus community. These reviewers will, again, focus on indicators of your child's academic potential, personal qualities, their pursuit of passions, and the results of those efforts. They may debate admitting your child, discussing their strengths and weaknesses among the group, and review supporting materials before making their final decision.

Step 4: Decision

After the review process is over, the admissions committee will use their reviews to decide whether to admit, defer (Early Decision, Early Action), waitlist (Regular Decision), or simply deny your child's application. If your child is admitted, their application's journey will be over. They will likely receive an offer of admission, along with any relevant financial aid or scholarship information.

If the decision is to defer, which typically happens with Early Decision or Early Action applications, that means the committee has decided not to admit your child early in the cycle but will reconsider the application alongside the other applications during Regular Decision. Your child may be asked to provide additional information or updates before a final decision is made.

If your child is waitlisted (Regular Decision), that means that their application has been placed on a list for future consideration if spots become available after admitted students decide which college they will be going to. A waitlist is basically a school's backup plan to fill any spots that open when admitted students decide to attend other schools. The admissions office may communicate with your child to provide additional information about the waitlist process and what steps, if any, they can take to strengthen their application. The admissions office may also provide updates to waitlisted applicants as the admissions process continues, such as notifying them of their status on the waitlist or providing information on the likelihood of admission.

If your child's application is denied, they will be notified of the decision and may also receive feedback on how to improve their application for future consideration. Feedback is uncommon and often must be requested on an individual basis. However, some colleges and universities have been known to offer feedback on applications, including:

- Harvard University: Harvard's admissions office offers feedback to a limited number of applicants who request it. The feedback is provided through an email or phone call and includes information on how the application could have been strengthened.

- University of California, Los Angeles (UCLA): UCLA's admissions office provides feedback to a small group of applicants who were not admitted but were deemed to have potential for future success at the university. The feedback is provided in the form of a letter and includes suggestions on how to improve the application for future consideration.

- Duke University: Duke's admissions office offers feedback to applicants who were waitlisted for admission. The feedback is provided through a phone call and includes information on why the application was not selected for admission and suggestions for strengthening the application.

While no one hopes for a denied application, it doesn't necessarily mean the end of that particular application's journey, as we'll discover later when discussing the appeal process. In the next chapter, we'll dig deeper on how to avoid a denied application in the first place, by learning from admissions officers from top US colleges about the most important factors that influence *their* seven-minute decision about your child.

CHAPTER 10

WHAT ADMISSIONS OFFICERS REALLY THINK

In the first nine chapters, I shared everything I know about the college admissions process. In this final chapter, I want to share some insights from admissions officers. I asked admissions officers from Carnegie Mellon University, New York University (NYU), and Stanford University for their thoughts.

WHAT IS THE BIGGEST MISCONCEPTION PEOPLE HAVE ABOUT THE COLLEGE ADMISSIONS PROCESS?

The biggest misconception about the admissions process is the role grades play in admissions decisions at highly selective institutions. Students are not admitted just because of their amazing grades. There is always something beyond the GPA or test score that the student will bring to the college community underlying the decision to admit. Of course, if a student is subpar academically when compared to the applicant pool, then the transcript could underlie the decision to deny that application.

There is no formula to get accepted. There is no guarantee for a student in the top of the class to be admitted. It is a competitive marketplace where all the high-end students apply to the same universities. At each of the highly selective universities, they could admit the class ten times over from the applicant pool with the same outstanding academic profile for their incoming class.

WHAT ARE THE BIGGEST MISTAKES STUDENTS MAKE WHEN COMPLETING THEIR COLLEGE APPLICATIONS?

Less is more! When a student puts too much information it takes away from what's truly meaningful for them. Listing too many activities will dilute the strength of their application. A student shouldn't feel obligated to fill in all the boxes provided in the application. Follow the instructions in the application, for example, if the school asks for two letters of recommendation, do not send three.

I love an essay where I learn more about the student rather than their research projects or activities already listed. These essays are not meant to be a narrative version of the extracurricular section of the application, but in many cases, this is what they become. Instead, students should focus on augmenting something already in the file; sparking the reader's interest in whatever it is that matters to the student. It's so fun and rewarding when you read an application and you feel you really know the student by the end.

WHAT MAKES AN APPLICATION STAND OUT FROM THOSE OF OTHER STUDENTS WITH SIMILAR QUALIFICATIONS?

Students who weave their voice throughout their essays tend to do better. Many admission officers will suggest students ask friends and family to review their essays prior to submission and pose the following question: "If you found this essay on the ground, without my name on it, would you know that it was mine?" This ensures the essay is personal and contains the student's voice. It's obvious to a reader when the student is authentic, sincere, and has done something unique. Don't try to write what you think will impress the admissions staff. Instead, write about what is important to you.

IN WHAT CIRCUMSTANCE WOULD YOU ADMIT A STUDENT WITH A LESS-THAN-PERFECT GPA OVER A STUDENT WITH A BETTER GPA?

It could be a variety of reasons. It may be the student made a significant impact in their community, received excellent test scores, or had other obligations (taking care of siblings, job to assist with financial family issues) that still demonstrated their potential for academic success.

Another common example of when a "less-than-perfect" GPA might win out is if that student took significantly more challenging courses than the "perfect" GPA student at that school. Perhaps, there is another component of that student's application that is compelling to the institution such as excellence in an extracurricular activity or connection to the institution. In most cases, however, that "less-than-perfect" GPA at a highly selective institution means maybe a single B or B+ (that's still a pretty good GPA!). At the end of the day, this is just one component of a completed application.

HOW IMPORTANT ARE STANDARDIZED TEST SCORES WHEN CONSIDERING AN APPLICATION?

As many schools have gone test-optional, standardized test scores are an additional way students can show they are ready for college-level course-work if they are confident in getting a good score. If a student feels standardized testing is not an area of strength and knows none of the schools they are applying to require standardized testing, it might be best to focus on other areas of the application and not spend the resources on an optional component. Even before highly selective institutions went test-optional, there was little conversation about a student's test score unless it was below the institution average.

Be strategic in whether you are going to submit your test scores. If possible, review your own school's data and search for the common data set for the specific college. If you are in the top 25th percentile, it's recommended to submit your test scores.

WHAT WOULD YOU CONSIDER A GOOD STRATEGY TO GAIN ADMISSION TO YOUR SCHOOL?

Apply Early Decision, meet with a representative if possible, and visit campus to ensure that this is the institution you'll want to attend.

Students should genuinely explore areas they are interested in and get involved in their communities as they feel is best—whether that is starting a new club, finding a part-time job, competing with athletic teams, or helping around at home with younger siblings—when students genuinely engage in their lives, the application becomes stronger.

HOW IMPORTANT ARE EXTRACURRICULAR ACTIVITIES AND WHAT DO YOU LOOK FOR IN THIS AREA?

Extracurricular activities are very important, but as stated above—it doesn't necessarily mean running for student body president. Students should find pockets of their communities that are personally meaningful and let their genuine interests drive the way they spend their time. Readers look for long-term engagement and possibly how the activity relates to the major they are interested in pursuing. Again, it's important the student is involved in whatever activity because they generally enjoy it and not because they want to showcase it for an admissions officer.

WHAT COURSES DO HIGH SCHOOL STUDENTS NEED TO TAKE TO GAIN ADMISSION TO YOUR SCHOOL?

Students will want to take the most rigorous courses offered at their high school, especially in the area that they want to pursue. For example, a student wanting to go into engineering should be taking a challenging math and physics curriculum.

The one requirement students tend to struggle to meet is the second language requirement as this varies from school to school. Taking three or more years of a second language will satisfy most requirements.

WHAT DO YOU LOOK FOR IN A RECOMMENDATION LETTER?

Most letters of recommendation are standard. A strong letter of recommendation will talk about how that student made a difference in the classroom, encouraged peers, led class discussions, went beyond expectations, and fostered an improved learning environment for all. When a teacher describes a significant difference in class on a day the student was absent, it's generally a strong letter.

WHAT DO YOU LOOK FOR IN AN APPLICANT'S ESSAYS?

This is an opportunity for the student to have a voice in the application. I want to feel like the student is reading the essay to me in my office instead of me just reading it on my screen. I would recommend keeping the essay to a single topic, don't reiterate activities and accomplishments, and don't overlook the importance of the supplemental essays. Sometimes, these are even more important than the personal statement!

IF YOU'RE ON THE FENCE ABOUT AN APPLICANT, WHAT DO YOU LOOK FOR TO GET YOU TO "YES?"

If an applicant is on the fence, those reviewing the application may ask for an additional opinion or re-review the entire application to ensure all information is captured before deciding.

IF YOU COULD GIVE SOMEONE WHO DREAMS OF ATTENDING YOUR SCHOOL ONE PIECE OF ADVICE, WHAT WOULD IT BE?

The reality of highly selective admissions is that very few students are ultimately admitted and students that don't get the decision they are hoping for usually had nothing wrong with their application. College will be an incredible time of learning and growth regardless of which institution a student attends because of how that student chooses to engage with the campus community. Ultimately, a university is not going to define you. You will be successful and grow at any college you attend!

That's the view from the admissions side of the process. Next, we'll look at some secret strategies that your child can also use to boost their chances of admission to an Ivy or other highly selective US school.

CHAPTER 11

SECRET STRATEGIES

Up until this point, we've been focusing on what I call "front door" strategies to help your child get accepted to a top US college or university. By "front door," I mean strategies derived from the application itself. Helping your child discover and develop their passions, choosing the best courses to help them meet their goals, writing a strong essay, and soliciting powerful letters of recommendation are all steps toward developing your child into a strong candidate with a compelling application.

There are, however, other ways a student can boost their chances of getting into their dream school that have nothing to do with their application.

There are "back door" admissions strategies, where students get admitted to a school that would otherwise be beyond their reach because their parents donate a building or set up a massive endowment. Similarly, there are students who will get extra consideration simply because they're a legacy (meaning their parent or other close relative went to the school), and maybe that relative has been actively involved with the school. If those kinds of options are available to your child (and you), there's certainly no reason not to employ them. Unfortunately, these strategies aren't available to most people reading this book.

You're probably also aware of some "side door" strategies, like the ones that were used during the infamous "Varsity Blues" scandal in 2019. In case you somehow escaped that headline-topping story, a group of thirty-three affluent parents were accused of paying a shady "college consultant" to get their kids admitted to several top-tier American schools...by any means necessary. The FBI discovered those means included boosting students' test scores through blatant cheating and by falsifying athletic portfolios on high school sports teams while bribing college coaches to recruit these faux players as elite athletes. Ultimately, over fifty people went to jail for the scheme. The list included the college counselor who masterminded the scandal, his employees, several coaches, officials from top schools like USC and Yale, and dozens of parents—including two TV stars!

At Ma Academy, we do not recommend employing any of these side-door strategies to help your child get into their dream school, and we strongly advise you to avoid any college counselor who does. That means doing your research in advance, and saying no to any counselor who:

- Illegally boosts test scores via strategies such as providing answers in advance, lying about a medical condition to secure extra time, bribing proctors, making corrections to the test before submission, or having someone else take the test

- Offers to write students' essays

- Encourages students to lie on their application by making up stories or experiences to make the application "more interesting"

That said, there are still a few little known side-door strategies that are both ethical and completely legal. First, if your child doesn't get into their dream school, there is always the option to start at a less-selective school with plans to transfer. Additionally, they can research which majors are least popular at their school and apply to a program that is hungry for students (hint: they can always change their major later!). On the more obscure end, a group of Ivy League schools have developed a set of bachelor's degree programs designed to serve working adults, meaning this isn't an option for a freshman right out of high school, but for students who are a little further along in life. These programs offer a real chance to attend their dream school. Realize that at some schools, these programs may be different from the school's regular bachelor's degree, while others integrate these non-traditional students into the student body. If your child is interested, check with the individual school to see what they offer, how long a potential student needs to be in the workforce (a single gap year, or more?) and any other requirements.

Some top colleges, like my own alma mater Columbia University, offer what are called 3-2 or 4-2 "dual degree" programs that allow students to earn a B.A. or BS from an "affiliated" college plus a BS in engineering from Columbia. In this scenario, the engineering department "partners" with a list of other, generally less-selective schools—Columbia partners with about 100 different colleges! The program is rigorous, but it provides students an alternate path to an Ivy League degree. Many schools offer these "cross-enrollment" opportunities, also called "consortiums."

There is not enough space to list all these opportunities here, but if your child has their heart set on a specific school, make sure to investigate every possible path to admission to that school beyond simply trying to kill it on their applications (not that they should skip that step!). Elite colleges in general are making more of an effort to serve non-traditional students, so explore every avenue that may lead to your child's dream school, including how affiliations with other, less-selective colleges may provide the side door your child is looking for.

Next Steps

Take some time to research the various avenues of admission that are available at your child's dream schools. Look for other schools that may be affiliated and any special programs the school may offer. If you're really motivated, get on the phone with someone from the admissions office and ask if they offer any alternate paths to admission and if they might be right for your child.

In our next and final chapter, we'll look at what to do when your child's decision letter arrives.

(ALMOST) EVERYTHING YOU NEED TO KNOW ABOUT COLLEGE SPORTS RECRUITING

When it comes to students playing on college sports teams, most people generally say "Oh, that student 'got recruited.'" The statement is passive, like it's something that just happens to a talented athlete. People assume scouts appear at games or matches and then, as if by magic, whisk the top players away to full-ride scholarships at big-name colleges with nationally ranked teams. In reality, getting recruited to play college athletics is a lot less of a fairy tale. It's the result of years of hard work off the field to make it happen. And that is actually very good news. It means your child doesn't have to be a superstar to play the sport they love in college. If you understand the opportunities that are available and how to approach them, you can help your child parlay their love for their sport into a chance to play for a college team.

I know this first-hand because I have helped countless student-athletes get recruited to top US schools. Through my experience partnering with many young athletes, I can guide you through this lengthy, multi-step process. By arming yourself with some basic knowledge of how recruitment works in this chapter, you can figure out how to make it work for you and your child, providing some control over their future college experience.

What Exactly Is Recruiting?

Generally, recruiting is the process of identifying, sourcing, screening, shortlisting, and interviewing candidates for positions within an organization. In college sports, the "organizations" are the school's various teams, and the "positions" are, literally, the positions available for students to play on those teams. The coaches looking to fill these positions all have different needs. Yes, most coaches want to win, and will focus on recruiting the best talent available in their sport *at their level* in order to maintain their school's ranking and reputation. But those words "at their level" mean more than you might imagine. What is "best" for one school may not be best for another. Coaches at academically rigorous schools need to balance their quest for top talent with students who also prove they will match their peers in the classroom. Depending on the year, different coaches have specific positions they need to fill as key players graduate or go pro. There are schools you and your child haven't even heard of fielding athletic teams that need players. It boils down to a matchmaking process that's not unlike finding the right college in the first place: looking for that perfect fit between the right student-athlete and the right program.

Is Your Child Good Enough to Play College Sports?

Many parents of high school athletes wonder whether their child has the stuff to make it on a college team. However, there's another, more important question that they (and you) need to answer first. Is your child *committed* enough to play college sports? Playing for a college team is very different from anything your child may have experienced in high school, or even at the elite club level. College sports training programs are rigorous, intense, and competitive. Your child probably won't be the best athlete on their team anymore. Nights and weekends will be spent practicing or traveling to games or matches. Holiday breaks from school mean more time to practice with their teammates instead of spending vacation at home hanging out with family and friends. As if that's not enough, there will be constant pressure to perform well academically to remain eligible to play. Ultimately, it may not be what your child has in mind for their college years, even if they really, really love their sport. If that is the case, most colleges have intramural or club sports, so your child can still experience the fun of competition without committing to the lifestyle of a student athlete.

In the end, only about seven percent of high school athletes participate in collegiate athletics. Those tend to be the student-athletes who have consistently taken their sport seriously, playing on multiple teams and attending additional training camps. US-based student-athletes who plan to play their sport in college traditionally attend special camps devoted to the sport in the summer and school breaks. These camps boost their skills and expose them to college coaches who could recruit them just a few years later. Camps like these help young athletes get noticed, build relationships, and become part of the larger community around their sport.

Sports camps in the US matter to Americans like summer academic programs matter to Asians. They are, for (American) student-athletes, essential college-preparation tools. Yes, there are always some students who discover their sport later in life and don't have the years of experience I'm talking about here, and the fact that your child hasn't been attending sports camp since age ten or twelve does not mean college sports are no longer a possibility. But now that you know how important sports camps are, if you know your child wants to play a sport in college, it's time to look for one nearby.

In college sports, "good enough" is a relative term because there are hundreds of college athletics programs to choose from, offering a range of different levels of play. The next step is to evaluate their skills to see what level of play is right for them. Your goal here should be to get an accurate, honest idea of your child's skill level, so you know which division (I-III) to target. After all, there's no point in setting your sights on a Division I school (more on that in a moment) if your child does not have the size or skill level to compete at that level. Focus on the right schools, take the right steps, and your child has a reasonable chance of seeing their dreams of playing college sports come true.

Your child's high school or club coach is a good first resource. Ask for an honest evaluation of your child's skill and ask for guidance about local programs. If you're in the US, their coaches may already have relationships with college coaches and be aware of their recruiting goals. There are also the aforementioned camps, showcases, and tournaments where your child can sign up for evaluation by college coaches. If your child plans to attend an event like this, ensure they reach out to the coaches in advance. Coaches often already have their eye on some players, and if that doesn't include your child, they will need to be proactive.

Some college counseling services, including Ma Academy, specialize in working with student athletes to help them target schools that meet both their academic and athletic goals. There are also paid recruiting services that focus specifically on evaluating student athletes and matching them with schools and programs that are a good fit.

Once you have a general sense of your child's level, do your research. Check the rosters of teams at target schools to evaluate the size, speed, and any other relevant stats of current players. In order to avoid going to all the trouble of getting recruited, only to end up in the wrong place, your child should strive to answer the following questions:

- Does the team need players for your child's position or event, or will they be relegated to the bench?

- Is your child a good "athletic fit" for the team, meaning they match the general size, speed, skill level, etc.? If they play a sport where players are ranked, like tennis or golf, is their ranking comparable to current players?

- Does the team recruit in your area? Nationally? Internationally?

- Who can your child contact to get on a team's radar?

Keep in mind that some college programs recruit a higher percentage of upperclassmen who transfer from junior colleges or other schools. Your child should aim to gather as much information as possible about their target schools' recruiting tendencies, tracking athletes at their position or event, and keeping count of who is graduating and who is coming in, to get a sense of which roster spots a coach will need to fill in the future.

The College Sports Divisions

Once you have a rough idea of your child's level, the next step is to come up with a list of target schools where their skills, size, and other stats match up with those of the current players. The schools will compete within different divisions (I-III), based on the level of play involved.

DIVISION I

NCAA (National Collegiate Athletics Association) Division I is probably what you think of when you think of college sports. It's the highest, most competitive level in college athletics, and the kind of school a future professional athlete will attend, since athletes who play for these schools, especially in televised sports like football and basketball, can become household names. Division I schools spend big money on their sports programs and expect their players to perform at an extremely high, almost professional level - after all, a lot of these games are on TV. They demand the biggest commitment from students in terms of training and travel. Athletics will become the bulk of their players' college experiences. Schools at this level routinely offer scholarships to top players and include many big names like Stanford University, Duke University, University of Virginia, Auburn University, and Northwestern University.

DIVISION II

NCAA Division II is one division down, but still offers scholarships to players. This is a competitive division, but the training and competition is less intense, and the media spotlight is less bright. As a result, student-athletes get to spend a little more time and energy being students, and a little less time and energy being athletes. Division II schools tend to be smaller than Division I schools. Some examples include Seattle Pacific University, University of California at San Diego, and Bentley University.

DIVISION III

NCAA Division III schools do not offer athletic scholarships, although the level of competition is still very high. These schools are more focused on academics and may be a better fit for athletes who want an elite education as well as a chance to play their sport. Their practice seasons are shorter and the expectations of players are more balanced, given the rigor of the school's academic programs. Division III schools include many top academic institutions including MIT, Johns Hopkins University, University of Chicago, and Emory University.

NAIA

NAIA (National Association of Intercollegiate Athletics) is a good option for students who want to play college sports, but are equally, or possibly more, focused on having a specific academic experience. NAIA schools are smaller, private, and operate in a smaller community of just over 250 institutions. The level of competition is much more relaxed than at NCAA schools. Some NAIA institutions include Columbia College, William Jessup University, and St. Ambrose University.

NCJAA

NJCAA (National Junior College Athletic Association) teams will not be found at top US colleges because this division is limited to junior colleges. They are a good option for students who do not meet

NCAA eligibility requirements for whatever reason and are set on playing their sport in college. Playing for a junior college team and doing well can serve as a path to eventually play at a four-year college or university.

NCCAA

NCCAA (National Christian College Athletic Association) is exactly what it sounds like: an NCAA division that's limited entirely to Christian schools. Therefore, these schools should appeal to students who love their sport and prefer to go to school in a specifically Christian environment. The NCCAA offers scholarships at the Division I level, but not Division II level. Indiana Wesleyan University and Trinity Christian College are examples of NCCAA schools.

WHEN DOES RECRUITING START?

Officially, college coaches at Division I and II schools are not allowed to reach out to prospective players until after June 15th of their sophomore year or after September 1st of their junior year. However, like almost everything we've discussed in this book thus far, recruitment of the most elite athletes begins during freshman year, or even earlier. The major US athletic programs are perpetually on the hunt for top talent, and if your child fits into that category, programs *will* send scouts to your child's game or at least view their film. By freshman year, a student who is already a top prospect, meaning they're already playing at a competitive varsity level and have led their teams to large all-state or similar titles, will likely be ready to start the recruiting process.

In fact, the recruitment process may start without your child even being aware that it's happening. While college coaches aren't permitted to contact players before the end of their sophomore/beginning of junior year, they are always looking at and evaluating prospective players who are younger, sometimes as early as middle school. They will reach out to high school and club team coaches and may even let them know that your child is being recruited. That means, if your child wants to play for a college team, they should aim to get on these coaches' radars sooner rather than later. College coaches may not be allowed to contact them personally, but your student can reach out via email or send a video whenever they feel ready. Be aware: even if your student sends an email, they shouldn't expect a response until the rules say it's okay.

This is a key point I want to take a moment to stress: even if your student-athlete has taken a little longer to find their footing, that doesn't mean they should rule out playing their sport in college if that's what they want. For every LeBron James, who was a phenomenon since he could dribble a basketball, there's a Michael Jordan, who didn't even make his varsity squad in high school. If your child is more of a late bloomer, or if they're not positive they even want to be a college athlete, waiting a little longer to jump into the recruiting pool is perfectly fine. Just be aware there will be some trade-offs. Waiting may eliminate the highest-tier programs from consideration, as other, equally talented students who start earlier may nab those spots. Waiting will almost certainly mean your child will work harder during their shortened recruitment period. And if your child hopes to play at the NCAA Division I or II level, you're going to need to start the process sooner rather than later. The athletes we work with usually start the recruiting process before the beginning of junior year, but it's never too early for your child to research colleges and rosters and update their video so they're ready to roll when coaches are allowed to make contact.

How Recruiting Works

Unless you were a college athlete yourself (and even if you were), you may not understand how college recruiting works. It's a complex process, so allow me to take a few minutes to familiarize you with the five steps college coaches follow and what you and your child should be doing to maximize their opportunities at each step.

STEP 1

Coaches consider a large pool of potential recruits, identifying prospective athletes who meet their basic requirements (height, weight, position, graduation year, academic record, etc.). Coaches find these potential athletes in a variety of ways. They utilize recruiting media websites like 247Sports or Rivals.com and attend camps and showcases (as discussed above) where student athletes play in hopes of being "scouted." They also find athletes via recommendations from current coaches, direct contact from the student athletes themselves, and third-party recruiting services that connect athletes with the right coaches at the right schools. The number of students who make it through the initial evaluation depends on the sport and size of the program with some Division I football teams having 7,500 student-athletes or more on their initial lists.

If your child is an athlete hoping to be recruited, this is the period where they should put together a list of schools that fit their athletic and academic needs. Start by casting a wide net like coaches do when they look for recruits, looking at every school that meets their basic criteria, then narrowing the field to the schools and programs that are the best fit. If there is a camp or a showcase hosted by a coach at any of these schools, your child should aim to attend. If they can't make it to camp, they can still email the coaches or reach out via social media to get on their radar. Remind your child to include relevant information the coach will need to evaluate them, such as stats and highlight videos.

STEP 2

Now, coaches begin reaching out to prospective recruits via questionnaires and invitations to showcases to determine who is interested in playing for their team. If your student passes the first evaluation, they will be contacted by the department to collect additional information. Here, your child will answer some basic questions about their qualifications and interest. There will be additional evaluations as coaches continue to narrow down the field of potential recruits.

If your student athlete receives any of these expressions of interest from an athletic program, make sure they respond with a heartfelt, personalized, "thank you" to the coach. Mail or email from a college coach means that coach is interested in learning more about your child, so your child should make the most of the opportunity. The more your student forms relationships with potential coaches, the better your student will do in the recruiting process. Just like admissions officers, coaches want to see what your child will add to their program when compared to other, similarly qualified players.

If your child is not contacted by any coaches, again, that doesn't mean their dreams of playing college sports are over. They can take initiative and jumpstart the process on their own. Have them email coaches at the schools they are interested in, introducing themselves, detailing their achievements both on and off the field (or court or course or track), and explaining why they are interested in that school and their program. This email should express your child's passion for their sport and interest in the specific team they hope to join.

STEP 3

If your child makes it to this point, the coach will start digging deeper into who your child is, including their athletic ability, academic record, and personal character. They may contact your child, ask their current coaches about their performance, and, in the best cases, request a recommendation. They may also show up at a tournament or showcase where your student-athlete is playing to see them in action or personally invite them to a camp. Coaches make both official and unofficial visits as they compile a strong list of possible recruits for their program. After this rigorous round of evaluations, they narrow the field again to a ranked list of anywhere from a dozen to a few hundred athletes, depending on the sport and division.

If your child's inbox is empty at this stage, encourage them to reach out to the coaches at the schools that meet their criteria by email or social media and make their case for why they deserve consideration. Remember that phrase *meet their criteria* when your child is contacting coaches. Your child should NOT simply shoot off an email to the coaches of the top five teams in their sport. The best part of recruitment is matching the right player to the right school. With so many different divisions and levels in college sports, there may be a place for your child to pursue their passion that neither of you are even aware of. The better you do your research (or your child does *their* research), the better the chances you will find the right match.

Besides emailing coaches themselves, your child can also ask their current coaches to reach out to college coaches on their behalf. Remember, whoever makes contact should include your child's most recent athletic and academic stats and videos. You can also schedule a visit to the school and let the coaches know your child will be there and would like to meet.

STEP 4

This step can begin as early as June 15th of your child's sophomore year or September 1st of their junior year, depending on the sport. Keep in mind that Division II and Division III schools typically wait to extend offers until an athlete's senior year. Coaches use their ranked list to extend offers to student athletes. How exactly this happens depends on the coach and the program, but most programs simply go down the list from top to bottom, making offers until all the open spots are filled. Be aware that a prospective coach may still invite your student-athlete to campus for an interview even after they get an offer, so be prepared for that possibility.

An important part of Stage 4 is understanding the offers that can be made by coaches.

- **Verbal offer:** non-binding and possible during any stage of the process. A verbal offer is exciting, but the fact that the offer is non-binding means anyone can back out for any reason (or no reason) at any time. That means the verbal offer a coach made your child at camp when they were a superstar freshman may not hold up when a more talented prospect pops onto the school's radar junior year.

- **Official offer:** binding and must follow NCAA guidelines. This results in a formal, legally binding National Letter of Intent, most likely during their senior year.

Once all the offers have been made and accepted, your student will join a recruiting class of anywhere from two to thirty fellow student athletes, depending on the school and the sport.

STEP 5

This final stage is when your student officially signs to play with a specific coach and school. This typically happens after a verbal offer and an official offer have been extended and accepted by your child. When your student signs the official offer, they must still meet the eligibility requirements set forth by their sport, school, and division.

Every school has its own eligibility requirements, including academic requirements, that a student-athlete must meet to be admitted and eligible to play, and each association also has its own, slightly different requirements. However, they all basically mean the same thing: if you want to play the game, you must make the grades. This includes both high school grades to be admitted and college grades to remain eligible to play. This can help a student-athletes applying with a strong GPA and high standardized test scores differentiate from a similarly talented competitor.

If your student athlete meets their goal and signs with a school, remind them that they absolutely must maintain their GPA and complete all required courses. If their grades drop below a certain threshold, they will be deemed ineligible to play. This leaves both your student and their new coach in a tough situation and may result in your child losing their spot on the team. If there is any chance your child may not meet their academic eligibility requirements, meet with their counselor immediately to formulate a plan to remedy the situation.

Overall, these five steps represent how coaches approach recruitment. Importantly, this is not a process that depends only on the coach – during any of the early steps your child can (and should) reach out to schools they are interested in proactively to get the recruitment ball rolling (no pun intended).

Six Major Myths About the Recruiting Process

At this point, you should have a clearer understanding of the process and what you and your child can do to make it work for them. However, before I close out this chapter, I want to address the most common myths about college sports recruiting and dispel them once and for all.

MYTH #1: ATHLETES GOOD ENOUGH TO PLAY COLLEGE SPORTS WILL AUTOMATICALLY GET RECRUITED.

This myth tops the list because it may be the single-biggest misconception about recruitment. Obviously, if your child is a nationally-recognized superstar, coaches are going to come calling. Most college athletes, however, were neither scouted as high schoolers nor "invited" to play for their college teams. Coaches are busy, recruiting is not their only responsibility, and they can't possibly be aware of every potential athlete out there who may be a perfect fit for their school. This is why it's crucial for your child to be proactive when it comes to getting recruited. To increase their chance of playing college sports, student-athletes should research programs, attend camps and showcases, discuss goals with current coaches, update highlight videos, and contact college coaches at target schools.

MYTH #2: YOU CAN COUNT ON YOUR CHILD'S COACH TO GET THEM RECRUITED TO A COLLEGE TEAM.

Can your child's coach help them get recruited to a college team? Absolutely. Is it a normal part of their job that they spend considerable time and effort on? Probably not. Many high school and club coaches have additional other "day jobs" unrelated to their coaching duties. They simply do not have the time to match every player who has the talent and dedication to play in college with the right coaches and schools in addition to everything else they do. You and your child can certainly ask their coaches for help, especially when it comes to connecting with local programs and coaches, but the bulk of the work should be done by (possibly you and) your child.

MYTH #3: THE RECRUITING PROCESS DOESN'T START UNTIL JUNIOR YEAR.

While coaches aren't allowed to initiate contact with student athletes until the end of sophomore year, that doesn't mean they aren't evaluating, considering, and maybe even planning to extend offers to high school freshmen and sophomores. College coaches are always looking for their next star players, regardless of whether those players have reached "recruitment age." If your child is serious about getting recruited, the best time to start preparing is, of course, right now. Don't advise them to wait for the offseason or delay into the future because there is nothing to be gained from sitting on the sidelines while other students are already playing the game.

MYTH #4: YOUR CHILD CAN CALL A DIVISION I COACH ANY TIME.

I'll be honest, this one isn't entirely a myth… Your child can certainly call or email a Division I coach if they want to. However, as of April 2019, if your child does not fit the right age parameters, these coaches cannot answer. To curb early recruiting, the NCAA Division I Council instigated a rule stating that coaches cannot accept calls from potential recruits until after June 15th (or September 1st) of their sophomore year. There is no rule, however, that bars student athletes of any age from calling, emailing, or sending video to get and stay on a coach's radar. Your child should proceed accordingly.

MYTH #5 – YOUR CHILD CAN PAY AN UNOFFICIAL VISIT TO A DIVISION I COACH WHENEVER THEY WANT.

Again, not entirely true. Potential recruits interested in Division II, Division III, NAIA and junior college recruitment can visit any school or coach at any time, as many times as they want to. However, when it comes to the prestigious NCAA Division I, no recruiting conversations are allowed until August 1st of a student's junior year of high school. Again, if your child is interested in making an unofficial visit to a Division I school before that point, there is no rule in place to stop them. They can still check out the campus, just not the coach. The exceptions to this rule are Division I football and women's basketball, in which coach contact during unofficial visits is still allowed.

MYTH #6: STUDENTS WHO AREN'T RECRUITED CAN ALWAYS "WALK-ON" LATER.

Maybe you've seen a movie where a high school athlete appears at a practice session out of the blue, beats every single player on the roster, dazzles the coach, and wins a spot on the team. Unfortunately, this rarely happens in real life. Yes, walk-on offers do happen, but they usually happen to "preferred" walk-ons, students who failed to earn an invitation to join a team during recruitment but are already known to the coach. That's why, even if your child fails to win a spot during recruitment, they should remain in contact with the coach.

Some coaches do keep spots on their roster open for players who they recruited but did not sign to become a walk-on later, but again, this is very rare, especially at the highest levels of college sports.

Recruitment for International Athletes

If you are based outside the US and your child dreams of playing for a US college or university, know that there are plenty of opportunities for international students to pursue their sport while getting a college education. Currently, there are more than 20,000 international students competing across the three divisions of the NCAA alone. However, to compete at a US school, an international recruit must go through the same process outlined throughout this chapter with a few additional hurdles.

The first hurdle is cultural. America, as a country, is crazy about sports. Americans attend sports camps, can easily visit and connect with local coaches, and their high school and club coaches may be more knowledgeable about the recruitment process. If your child is competing outside the US and they want to play college sports, they will need to do whatever they can to level the playing field, so to speak. If you have the means to send your child to an American sports camp, I recommend doing so as soon as you know your child is serious about their plan to pursue college sports, for as many summers as you can afford. If not, seek out whatever opportunities you can find closer to home.

Still, plenty of American colleges do recruit international athletes, often from countries that have strong programs in those sports. Tennis, track and field, ice hockey, golf, field hockey, soccer, water polo, and basketball have the highest numbers of international athletes playing at the college level in the US This means college coaches in these sports may be more familiar with the process of recruiting international athletes, or even more likely to offer international students a chance at an open roster spot.

Sports with the lowest rates of international athletes include football, baseball, softball, and wrestling. This means college coaches in those sports may not be experienced in recruiting international athletes, but it doesn't mean your child has no chance of getting recruited if they play one of these sports. It just may make the recruiting process more difficult, unless they are an elite athlete who is already well known internationally.

Whatever sport your child plays, if they hope to play at an American college or university, they will need to put some extra time, energy and effort into what is already a time-consuming and complex process. Here are some basic guidelines for international students to follow:

1. Learn the lay of the land. Research the best colleges for student athletes and the best schools in your child's sport. Familiarize yourselves with the division levels, programs of interest, and additional deadlines. Remember that attending college in the US could be a bit of a culture shock for any international student, so take time to explore what it means to be a student in America in addition to becoming a student-athlete.

2. Make sure your child is eligible to play. If your child hopes to attend and play for an NCAA or NAIA school, they will need to register with the division's Eligibility Center and check that they meet all requirements, academic and otherwise. You may need translated and certified documents verifying your child's grade, test scores, and transcripts.

3. Help your child create a list of target schools. Remember to consider not only your child's level as an athlete, but the type of school they want to attend, including location, climate, school size, culture, degree of rigor and selectivity, etc. There are many, many options across all divisions of college sports, so encourage your child to think about the overall college experience they hope to have. Then, once they narrow down their list, start contacting coaches. Remember, those coaches likely already have local athletes on their radar, so the earlier they can be introduced to your child, the better the chance your child will succeed.

Next Steps

No matter what grade your child is in, if they are considering college sports, now is the time to start planning for recruitment. If you and your child follow the steps and processes outlined in this chapter, chances are good your student-athlete is the exact player a college coach somewhere is hoping to add to their roster.

In our next and final chapter, we'll look at what to do when your child's decision letter arrives.

CHAPTER 13

WHAT'S NEXT?

By this point, you and your child should be armed with the knowledge you need to create a strong application to the schools that best match their abilities, goals, and dreams. Still, when your child is applying to elite colleges, especially colleges that have an acceptance rate under 5 percent, the outcome is never guaranteed. Winning admission to a top college or university is supposed to be hard, that's what makes these schools so prestigious and desirable in the first place. But it also means a rock-solid application does not always guarantee acceptance. This leaves us with one final phase to deal with in the college application process: formulating a plan to deal with each possible application decision.

Once your child's college application has been received, it will enter the admissions system at that school. Your child will probably be notified via email that their application has been received and given access to an online *admissions portal* where they can track their application's status. Some smaller schools don't have admissions portals and may communicate with applicants by email, snail mail, and even phone. Make sure you and your child know what to expect from each institution they have applied to.

By this point your child will know if they have been accepted to their ED school, or if they have been moved to the RD pool. This chapter will focus solely on RD outcomes, which are announced in early spring. Your student will be notified in advance of the date when they can log into the admissions portal to view their decision status. There are three possible outcomes: *accepted*, *waitlisted*, or *rejected*.

Let's look at these one at a time.

Acceptance

If your child is accepted to their dream school or any of their target schools, congratulations to both of you! They will likely get this news through the school's admissions portal or email. That's not *quite* as exciting as it was in the old days, when you discovered you were accepted to a school by opening the mailbox to find an oversized envelope stuffed with admission materials and college swag. The element of surprise may be gone, but don't worry! That same thick package should arrive shortly after your child receives the official thumbs up.

FINANCIAL AID FACTS

If your child has applied for financial aid, they should be notified of any aid they have received around the same time they receive their acceptance letter. Colleges and universities do this so families can consider their aid offer when making a final decision. We did not go into the process of how to apply for or obtain financial aid in this book, but if paying for your child's education may be an issue, make sure you research the FAFSA (Free Application for Federal Financial Aid), the CSS Profile (College Scholarship Service Profile), and any scholarships or grants offered by your child's target schools ahead of time. There are also all kinds of public and private scholarships designed to help almost every type of student, so do some research and get your child started on those applications ahead of time. Luckily, they may be able to re-use some of their college application materials in the process.

Many colleges provide online access to yet *another* secure portal where students can view and manage their financial aid information. The initial notification, which may also arrive via email or snail mail, will explain how much financial aid your child will receive and what form it will be in (grants, scholarships, loans, work-study, etc.). It will typically provide information on any deadlines or requirements that your child needs to fulfill to accept or decline the financial aid offer. Generally, this includes submitting additional documents, signing acceptance forms, and completing counseling sessions.

Students typically have until May 1st to commit to a school, and by *commit*, I mean making an actual deposit of real American money to secure their place in the next class. If your child is accepted to multiple colleges or is waiting to hear from a specific dream school, they have until the end of April to decide where to go. Some schools have different deadlines, or what's called "rolling acceptance," so be sure you and your child are familiar with each school's specific process and what needs to be done when to hold their spot in the incoming class.

The Waitlist

If your child is notified that they are on a school's wait-list, it means that the college is not ready to give them a spot now, but may have space for them when students who have been offered admission choose other schools instead. Your child may learn they've been waitlisted the day admission decisions are posted whether through the portal or email.

The waitlist notification will usually include instructions and information about what your child should do next. If they are interested in the school, they should immediately respond to the waitlist offer and indicate their continued interest in being considered for admission. Your child may be asked to reply through the online portal or online form. Regardless of what's required, if your child is waitlisted for a school they hope to attend, encourage them to take this opportunity to make their case. The notification will ask your child to update their application with any significant experiences or awards since they applied. Your student should absolutely take advantage of this opportunity to provide an update and express their continued interest in attending the institution. Finally, they should check the school's website or contact the admissions office to find out if the school will let them know their position on the list. Most schools are willing to share that information, and it can be valuable in helping your child decide their next steps.

After your child submits any required items, they will need to wait until after May 1st, when already admitted students must decide where they will be attending college. At this point, the school knows how many spots are remaining in the incoming class and can start admitting waitlisted students. This can, and often will, continue into the summer months. Many waitlisted students do get admitted to these schools, but it is never a guarantee and often fluctuates year to year.

My advice is to consider whatever admission offers your child does have and submit a deposit to their best-choice school. It's important to realize that waiting can be stressful and may not be worth the added stress if your child has admission offers from other schools they are equally excited about. If your child still wants to join the waitlist, that's fine too! The worst thing that can happen is your child will get into their dream school and you (or they) will be out anywhere from a few hundred to a thousand dollars. That's what I call a good problem to have. In the end, it's a small price to pay for the peace of mind of knowing your child can hold out for their dream school without losing their chance of going to *any* school.

Rejection

Rejection happens. When your child is competing with the best of the best for a spot at a school that admits less than twenty, ten, or even five percent of its applicants, even a perfect application may wind up in the "no" pile. If this happens to your child, it may be the first time they haven't gotten something they wanted, and taking the news can be hard. But rejection is a life experience everyone will have sooner or later. What matters here is what you and your child do next.

The first and most common option is for your child to go to the best school that did accept them. They can go in with a plan to apply as a transfer student to their dream school after a year or two, or simply commit to experiencing college and pursue their passion at their best-choice school, maybe with the goal of applying to graduate school at their dream school. Many, many students choose this path and wind up having incredible, positive college experiences that they wouldn't trade for anything.

The second option is to *appeal* the decision. Most colleges don't advertise this as an option; however, your child can contact the school and ask if there is any way they can appeal. If the school agrees, your child will be asked to demonstrate "grounds for appeal," like a mistake on the application or a major achievement that happened after their application was submitted. If your child is allowed to appeal, remind them that any achievement since their application was first submitted qualifies as "new," including personal growth. This should all be included in the *appeal letter* your child will be asked to write to explain their grounds for appeal. If your child gets an opportunity to write an appeal letter, they should make it clear that, if accepted, they will definitely attend the school (including specifics about why they chose that school), and demonstrate why they are a good fit and deserve admission.

WILL WRITING AN APPEAL LETTER WORK? NOT ALWAYS, BUT IT MIGHT.

Will it work? I wouldn't bet the farm on it. Students are rarely admitted to top schools on appeal. But there's always a chance your child's dream school is somebody else's second, third, or even last choice. College admissions can be a fluid process, so if your child is rejected from a school they have their heart set on attending, there's no harm in trying one last time. If they can manage to wrangle another chance to make their case and possibly get what they really want, why shouldn't they? Just make sure that, no matter how good they think their appeal letter is or how lucky they feel, they proceed as if the answer will be no. This means making a deposit to their second-choice school, or…

…your child can delay starting college and take a *gap year*.

Gap years (meaning a year off, typically between high school and college) are becoming more and more popular, to the point that there are now specific gap year programs your child can apply to and participate in. Those programs can make a huge difference in the strength of a college application. Imagine what your child's application would look like if they dedicated an entire year to their biggest passion: immersing themselves in it, gaining experience, and growing their skills and knowledge. If your child doesn't get into any schools they want to attend, *not* enrolling in college and spending what would otherwise be their freshman year doing something meaningful can pay off in the long run.

This is not a strategy to employ without a plan. Sitting around watching TV for a year isn't going to win your child admission to their dream school next time around. Neither is taking another year to study for and retake standardized tests to raise their scores. On the other hand, if there is something compelling your child can *do* that will add to their resumé and strengthen their application theme, a gap year may be a brilliant strategy. Just keep in mind that, if your child opts to decline their offers and take a gap year instead, they will have to restart the application process all over again in the fall. This may be tougher once they've graduated from high school, especially if they are living away from home. However, for the right student, a gap year can be a great way to gain valuable experience and learn new things outside the classroom.

WHAT IF MY CHILD GETS REJECTED BY EVERY SCHOOL THEY APPLIED TO?????

First of all, calm down. If you read this book and put it into practice with your child, including researching and targeting at least some schools that are likely to admit them, this is a highly unlikely scenario. If the unthinkable happens, enrolling in a local junior college with a plan to transfer or devoting a gap year to growing their skills are both solid options. But, again, if your child spent their high school years pursuing their passions and their college applications clearly expressed and illustrated this theme, you're not likely to need these backup plans.

CONCLUSION

Over the last thirteen chapters, I've shared everything I know, or at least a good overview of everything I know, about the admissions process at top US colleges. If you came across this book early enough in the college preparation process, you and your child will be able to identify their passions early, pursue them at a deeper level every year, and design a high school experience that will prepare your child for the future they want. By their senior year of high school, you and your child will be ready to express this growth and achievement in their college applications. Even if you picked up this book a little late, the information I shared should help you and your child zero in on their passions and modulate their remaining time in high school to support a coherent application theme. Wherever your child is in the process, having read this book will put them ahead of the game and give you an idea of what you need to focus on as your student approaches college.

It's a lot of work, but it will all pay off the moment your child logs into their admissions portal at one of their target schools and finds out they have been admitted. However, after all the screaming with joy and jumping up and down celebrating is over, you and your child will be left with something much more valuable than admission to a specific school.

The time and attention you give to guiding your child though this experience is a gift that will put them ahead of their peers and leave them feeling prepared for school, and for life. By helping your child find clarity about themselves, their passions, and their dreams in life, you will help them choose a college environment where they can thrive. Guiding your student through this process will provide your child with the ability to dream and make those dreams come true.

THE TIME AND ATTENTION YOU GIVE TO GUIDING YOUR CHILD THOUGH THIS EXPERIENCE WILL TEACH THEM SKILLS THEY WILL HAVE LONG AFTER COLLEGE.

That's something any parent can be proud of.

For more information about how my team and I can help your child prepare for admission to college, contact me at:
sma@leightonschool.com

ACKNOWLEDGMENTS

I am deeply grateful to everyone who contributed to the creation of this book on college admissions and recruiting. Without the generous support and insights of numerous individuals, this project would not have been possible.

First and foremost, I would like to express my heartfelt appreciation to all the admissions officers from various colleges and universities who graciously participated in the information sessions. Your valuable expertise and willingness to share knowledge have been instrumental in shaping the content of this book. Your dedication to guiding students on their educational journey is truly commendable.

Additionally, I extend my sincere gratitude to all the college coaches whose guidance has been vital to my understanding of the intricate recruiting process. Your passion for developing young talent and your commitment to fostering both academic and athletic growth have left a lasting impact on me. Your insights have enriched the narrative of this book and will undoubtedly aid countless students and athletes in navigating the complexities of college recruitment.

I would also like to thank my family and friends for their unwavering support and encouragement throughout this writing journey. Your belief in my abilities and your patience during long hours of writing are deeply appreciated.

Furthermore, I want to acknowledge the guidance and expertise provided by Lucy Chechik, Megan Colt, and Carlos Lecanda. Your constructive feedback and thoughtful suggestions have been invaluable in refining the ideas presented in this book.

Finally, to all the readers who have chosen to embark on this journey with me, thank you for investing your time and interest in this subject. It is my sincerest hope that this book will be of assistance to you and contribute positively to your college admissions and recruiting experiences.

With gratitude,

Sean Ma

Printed in the USA
CPSIA information can be obtained
at www.ICGtesting.com
JSHW021524110324
58997JS00004B/217

9 781642 259131